Quilt As-You-Go
FOR SCRAP LOVERS

12 Fun Projects
Tips & Techniques
Color & Piecing Strategies

JUDY GAUTHIER

C&T PUBLISHING
Another Maker Inspired!

Text and photography © 2023 by Judy Gauthier

Photography and artwork copyright © 2023 by C&T Publishing, Inc.

PUBLISHER: Amy Barrett-Daffin

CREATIVE DIRECTOR: Gailen Runge

SENIOR EDITOR: Roxane Cerda

EDITOR: Liz Aneloski

TECHNICAL EDITOR: Debbie Rodgers

COVER/BOOK DESIGNER: April Mostek

PRODUCTION COORDINATOR: Zinnia Heinzmann

ILLUSTRATORS: Aliza Shalit, Wendy Mathson, Kerry Graham

PHOTOGRAPHY COORDINATOR: Lauren Herberg

FRONT COVER PHOTOGRAPHY by Lauren Herberg of C&T Publishing, Inc.

SUBJECTS PHOTOGRAPHY by Lauren Herberg of C&T Publishing, Inc.;
INSTRUCTIONAL PHOTOGRAPHY by Judy Gauthier, unless otherwise noted

Published by C&T Publishing, Inc., P.O. Box 1456, Lafayette, CA 94549

Library of Congress Cataloging-in-Publication Data

Names: Gauthier, Judy, 1962- author.
Title: Quilt as-you-go for scrap lovers : 12 fun projects; tips &
  techniques; color & piecing strategies / Judy Gauthier.
Description: Lafayette, CA : C&T Publishing, [2023] | Summary: "Quilt
  as-you-go is the ultimate DIY sewing technique used to help make quilts
  uniquely your own. Along with the QAYG technique, there are color and
  piecing strategies and 12 fun projects included for quilters to utilize
  for making sensational scrappy quilts"-- Provided by publisher.
Identifiers: LCCN 2022031361 | ISBN 9781644032732 (trade paperback) | ISBN
  9781644032749 (ebook)
Subjects: LCSH: Patchwork--Patterns. | Quilting--Patterns. | Machine
  sewing--Technique.
Classification: LCC TT835 .G33177 2023 | DDC 746.46/041--dc23/
eng/20220812
LC record available at https://lccn.loc.gov/2022031361

Printed in China

10 9 8 7 6 5 4 3 2 1

Dedication

Since this book is educational, I would like to dedicate it to all the experienced teachers who carry on our craft. I would especially like to mention the men and women who are in their later years in life. These are the instructors with vast amounts of knowledge and experience. They know how a pattern will work or not work and why and how a fabric will behave in your hands. That kind of experience is invaluable.

Acknowledgments

I would like to thank Cathleen Roeder, my good friend of many years, for teaching me so much about the quilting process. She is a longarm quilter who has it all figured out. She has taught me much about thread and tension and how to choose a good design. I would also like to thank Sherry Purtell, Karen Haines, and Nancy Wszalek, who came to my aid when I was struggling to finish this book in time. Thanks also to my husband who got up from his desk multiple times while we were both working to take our golden retriever puppy outside. I couldn't have made deadlines without you. I would also like to thank Cindy Cody for keeping the shop afloat while I worked on this project. And thank you, Duncan, for being my constant companion and keeping my feet warm.

Contents

Reverse Churn Dash   82

Payson   86

Frank is
Always Wright   90

Mountains Majesty   96

Parlor Games   100

Tucson Sunset   106

Introduction

As the owner of a quilt shop, I hear it all. As an ICU nurse, I've seen it all, but we definitely won't go there.

What do you want as a quilter? Some quilters want to send their quilt to a longarm quilter. They are relieved when they don't have to worry about how to quilt their quilt. Some quilters feel they don't want to hand their quilt off to someone else. Rather, they feel that they have done it all by themselves. They've chosen the design and the fabric, lovingly constructed the blocks, and have done everything, right up to the point of layering. They don't want to hand it off to someone else. Most of us are a hybrid—we often want some parts of our quilts done by a longarm quilter. Sometimes, the additional cost of taking it to a longarm quilter is not ideal, and there are some quilts that we just want to be totally involved with from start to finish.

What happens when you have that deep desire to own your quilt from start to finish? You may want to quilt it yourself, but you may only have a home sewing (domestic) machine. Do you have to put the entire quilt into the throat of the sewing machine (the area between the needle and the body of the machine)? Can you quilt it in smaller sections?

Enter stage left ... quilt as-you-go.

This book will teach you how to quilt as you go. It is the ultimate fix for anyone who wants to quilt a quilt on a domestic sewing machine without using a quilting machine (either a longarm machine or a sit-down machine with an extra-large throat). Quilt as-you-go is a method for quilting a quilt in sections smaller than the entire quilt. After the sections are quilted, you then join them together.

There are multiple ways to quilt as-you-go and several techniques to use, and all of them are done on a domestic sewing machine. Quilt As-You-Go for Scrap Lovers will teach you how.

Quilting for Quilt As-You-Go

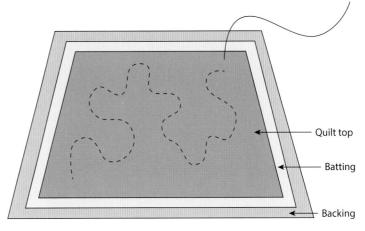

Quilt top

Batting

Backing

Note For the purposes of this book, *piecing* is the act of sewing small shapes together to create the top of a quilt and *quilting* is the act of stitching together the three quilt layers: the pieced top, the batting, and the backing.

There are two ways to quilt a quilt: You can quilt it by hand or you can quilt it by machine.

Piecing is usually done on a domestic home sewing machine. But quilting the sandwiched quilt top, batting, and backing of an entire quilt can sometimes be a challenge on a domestic sewing machine if the quilt is large.

The actual act of quilting as-you-go uses the same technique as quilting a large intact quilt; you're just working in smaller sections. Sectioning and joining the sections is the meat of the matter in the quilt as-you-go method.

Quilting can be done free motion with the feed dogs down or in straight lines with a walking foot. It can also be done by hand.

Let's discuss some quilting basics and terminology.

Free–Motion Quilting

Free-motion quilting is exactly what it sounds like. The quilter moves the quilt sandwich in all directions because the feed dogs of the sewing machine are lowered. Most sewing machines are equipped with the ability to lower the feed dogs so that they don't engage with the fabric. When they are down, you can move the quilt sandwich around in multiple directions without having to turn the entire quilt sandwich. It allows you to go back and forth and side to side. Under normal sewing situations, with the feed dogs up, the sewing machine will only let the fabric move forward or backward. Meandering, or stippling, is done with the feed dogs lowered.

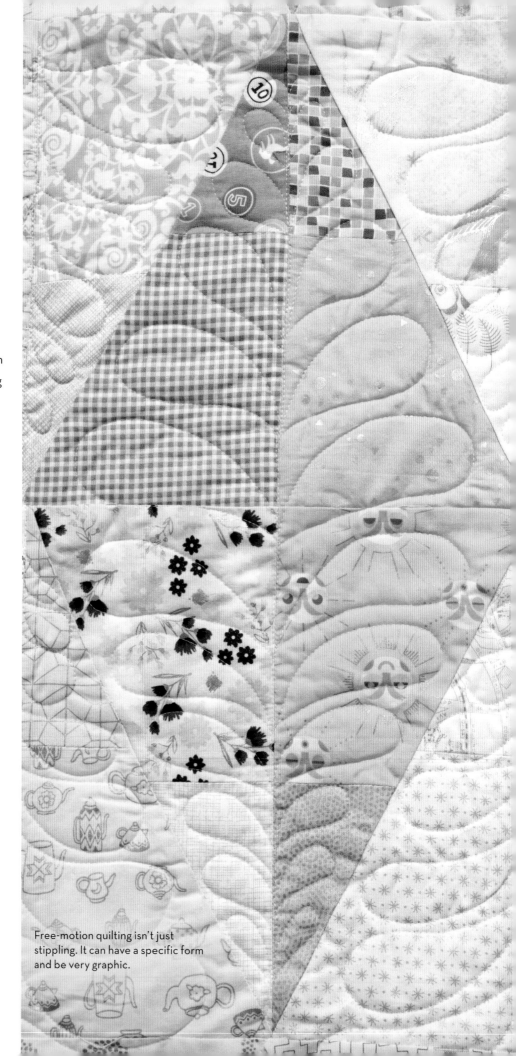

Free-motion quilting isn't just stippling. It can have a specific form and be very graphic.

Stitching Evenly Across the Quilt Surface

Quilt as-you-go is done in sections. I want to emphasize how important it is to have an even amount of quilting on each section of the quilt. Every section must be the same size and have approximately the same amount of quilting across the surface if you want the sections to be a consistent size after the quilting is finished. Look over your quilt with this in mind—you should be able to tell if it looks even.

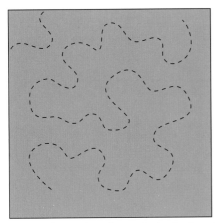 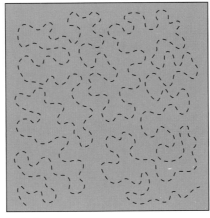

Left: Quilting is less dense. *Right:* Quilting is much denser.

Make certain that your sections have the same dimensions prior to quilting.

When you quilt a quilt sandwich, the dimensions change slightly. There is some taking in of the fabric. Therefore, it's very important to quilt all sections with the same density. If you have ever been to a quilt show and observed that a quilt appeared to be bowing in a particular section, it was because there was a portion of the quilt that was more heavily quilted than the rest. If one section of your quilt has dense quilting, not only will there be bunching and shortening of the materials within that section, but the additional thread will make that section heavier than the surrounding areas.

Start with equally sized sections and quilt each section evenly and you will be set up for success.

Sections are same size prior to quilting.

Note The exception to this rule is when you're doing quilt as-you-go for an on-point quilt (see On-Point Quilts, page 22).

Stitch Regulation

When you are free-motion quilting, you move the quilt around as the needle moves up and down and makes the stitches. Depending on your skill level and amount of practice, your stitches may be long and short and very uneven. That's because you aren't a machine! We're all human and may not be able to move the quilt at a consistent speed for the duration of quilting. Quilts are also heavy and create drag, so some stitches might be long and some might be short.

A **stitch regulator** regulates the stitch length as you are moving the quilt. When you are moving the quilt quickly, the machine speeds up, and vice versa. A stitch regulator is a computerized eye that sees the movement of the quilt and increases or decreases the speed of the stitches to help make them an even length.

Is it necessary to have a stitch regulator? No. If you practice free-motion quilting, the hand-eye coordination you develop will eventually replace any need for a stitch regulator. Some quilters I know never use one—they are just so practiced that they can do without. This takes many years of experience, but if you do free-motion quilting a lot, you too will become accomplished. The way that I taught myself and got lots of practice was by making a bunch of quilts for a homeless shelter. I could let go of any imperfections in my quilting, and I got a lot of practice.

Some stitches are smaller and some larger when a stitch regulator is not used.

Unsewing ... A Necessary Topic

This topic carries more weight in a book where actual quilting of the quilt sandwich is involved because tearing out the quilting is harder than tearing out piecing.

Once you have all three layers stitched together, you may not like the look of it. You may have had trouble with tension. You may just decide that you should rip it out. But in the words of a very experienced, very wise friend of mine who is a longarm quilter, "Be forgiving of yourself and let yourself get practice." If you don't start somewhere, you'll never get any better. And if you spend all your time ripping things out, you won't ever finish your project.

Whew. Glad to get that out of the way.

That being said, you're still going to want to undo your quilting at some point. It can be difficult to rip out quilting. Even though the stitches are going through three layers, you need only rip out stitches from one side of the quilt and the stitches will come out of all the layers.

There are several ways to attack this problem.

1. Seam rippers: These are handy little tools that have been around for a long, long time. There are a couple of different ways they can be used to remove quilting: from the outside, by picking at the stitches, or between the layers, by using the sharp inner curve.

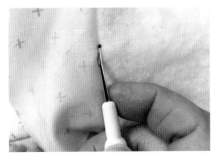

2. Rotary cutting blades: I can assure you that these are never anyone's first choice, but there are just times when nothing but a blade will work. If your stitches are too small to use a seam ripper, you're going to need to resort to a blade. I can remember my mother ripping things out using a razor blade. The old-fashioned razor blades had a covering over one edge to allow you to hold onto them. I'm afraid that rotary blades don't have this. If you're going to use them, *please, please* wear gloves. Also know that you are in danger of cutting your fabric. Always cut the stitches between the batting and the backing, never between the pieced front and the batting. If you accidentally cut the fabric—which is going to happen at some point when you're ripping out quilting—be sure to apply some form of fray retardant to the spot immediately. There are many different formulas made by different companies.

3. Tiny shavers: This is the best way I can think of to describe these tools without endorsing any one product. Using one of these is by far the best way to rip out quilting from a quilt sandwich. If you choose this approach, be sure to rip between the batting and the backing as you would with blades. If something is going to get damaged, let it be the back of the quilt rather than the front.

Yes, ripping is a necessary evil. You must have the courage to try something new and know that it won't be perfect. My best advice is to learn to live with a few imperfections.

Sectioning Your Quilts for Quilt As-You-Go

By now, you've figured out that quilt as-you-go involves quilting your quilt in sections. Instead of putting your blocks together and making an entire quilt top, with a quilt as-you-go quilt, you are working on one small section at a time.

There are multiple ways to section a quilt as-you-go quilt. The design and type of blocks in the quilt will determine which method to use. For the purposes of this book, I have given these sections names: columnar sections and quarter sections.

Columnar Sections

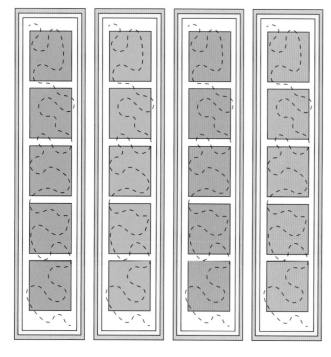

Dividing your quilt into vertical or horizontal columnar sections is the most common approach for sectioning. It is also the simplest. It is used on quilt tops that are built in rows or columns, and most quilt as-you-go quilts are put together this way. In the columnar method, instead of putting the entire quilt top together, you put one or several rows of the pieced top together and then stop. The sections can be made with rows or columns.

First, you need to determine how large each of your sections will be. Whether you attach two rows or columns and then make your quilt sandwich or whether you do each column or row separately is an individual choice. This will depend on your level of experience with sewing and quilting. It will also depend on your sewing machine. If you have a sewing machine with a fairly small throat, you will need to keep your sections fairly small. If you are not very experienced, you will need to keep your sections small. Keeping your sections small will allow you to maneuver your quilt sandwich within the throat. There will be some turning and rolling of the sandwich as you quilt.

Layering Columnar Sections

Layer each quilt top section with batting and backing to make the quilt sandwiches. The batting should be about 1″ larger than the pieced quilt-top section on all sides, and the backing should be about 3″ larger on all sides. This is a relative guideline; larger or smaller quilt-top sections may require different measurements.

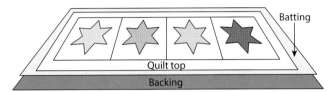

This is my typical preference; you just don't want to short yourself. The suggestion differs for some patterns in this book and from quilt to quilt. Standard-size, precut battings will sometimes work for a project but with only a few inches extra around each section.

Lay the backing down first, wrong side up. Lay the batting on top of the backing and then lay the pieced quilt top, right side up, on top of the batting. Smooth the layers from the center outward. There must be absolutely no puckering or bunching, and the batting and the backing must extend beyond the pieced top on all sides.

Basting Columnar Sections

Basting is quite possibly the most important part of the entire process. The quilt will only turn out as well as it's basted. Basting is quite possibly the most important part of the entire process. Oh, did I say that more than once? That's because I cannot emphasize this enough.

Some quilters love to use quilt-basting sprays. If you choose to do this, be sure to follow the instructions on the product. To spray baste, you spray the wrong side of the backing and the top side of the batting that touches the back of the pieced quilt top. Follow the instructions that come with the product for spraying and smoothing the layers.

> **Note** Personally, I don't like basting sprays. I think that the less we breathe in aerosolized particles, the better off we are.

I prefer to pin baste. If you're using safety pins and pin basting, your pins should be very close together and must puncture all three layers of the sandwich.

Start at the center of the quilt sandwich and insert a pin. Close the pin after you're certain that you have all three layers in the pin. Then, every 2″, insert another pin. Each time you put in 2 or 3 pins, smooth the layers outward from the center. Check to make sure you don't have any puckers or folds underneath by lifting and looking. Baste each section.

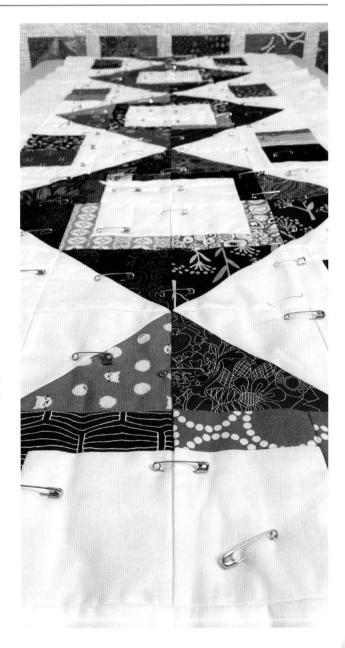

Quilting Columnar Sections

Quilt in your preferred manner, but don't forget to keep the tension even and the density of the quilting consistent between sections (see Stitching Evenly Across the Quilt Surface, page 9).

Roll the quilt sandwich section from one short end to the other. Unroll one end slightly and put it into the throat of the sewing machine with the unrolled section under the needle.

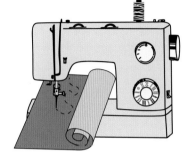

Quilt the first area, leaving at least ½" unquilted. You mustn't quilt all the way to the edges of the quilt

Quilt first area.

sandwich. The edge of each section is where you will join sections. If you quilt all the way to the edges, you won't be able to join the sections.

Stitch the quilt sandwich with the quilting design, then unroll the sandwich to expose the next area. Quilt the entire section, then repeat this process for all the sections of the quilt.

Joining/Seaming Columnar Sections

Joining the Quilt-Top Layers

Join the sections together after they are quilted.

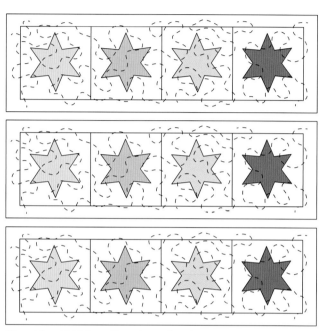

Stay at least ½" from the edges of each section.

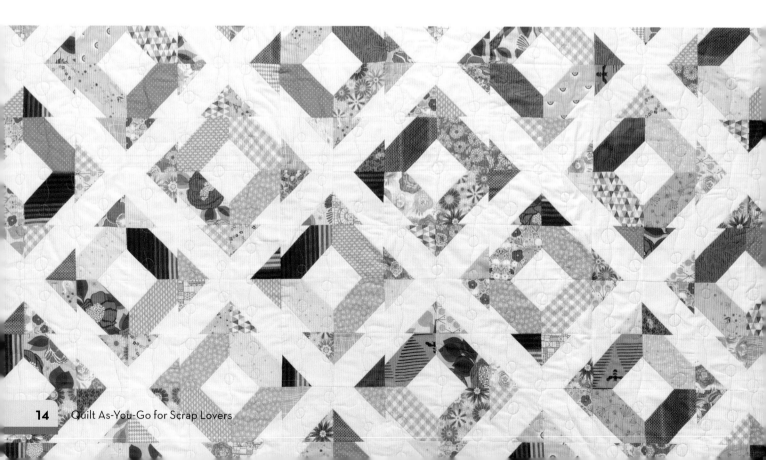

1. Stack 2 quilt-top sections, right sides together. Pin them together, matching all seams and leaving the batting and the backing free. The batting and the backing are not sewn during this step.

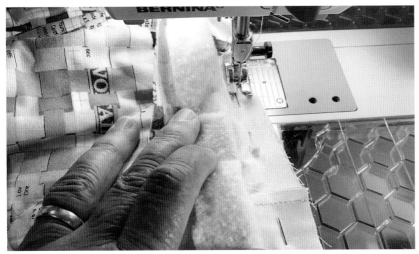

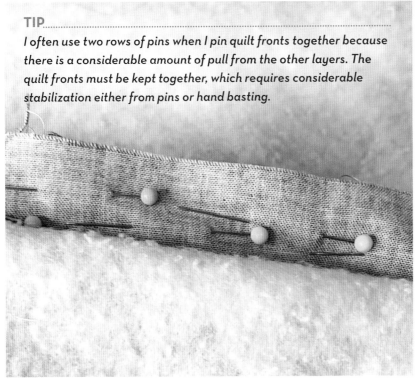

TIP
....

I often use two rows of pins when I pin quilt fronts together because there is a considerable amount of pull from the other layers. The quilt fronts must be kept together, which requires considerable stabilization either from pins or hand basting.

2. Stitch them with a ¼″ seam allowance.

3. Press the seam allowances, keeping the batting and the backing free.

Joining the Batting Layers

1. Carefully cut the batting on each side so that it meets over the seam.

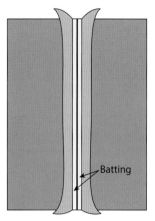

2. Whipstitch the batting edges together using piecing thread.

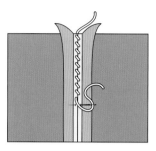

Joining the Backing Layers

1. Smooth the backing fabric of one section toward the center where the batting is stitched. Fold it back on itself with the fold lying along the seam of the batting. Press a crease into the backing.

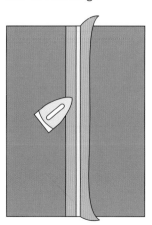

2. Cut along the crease. Fold the backing fabric of second section toward the center so it covers and extends 1½" beyond the cut edge of the first section's backing fabric. Mark a line with a marking tool and cut along the line.

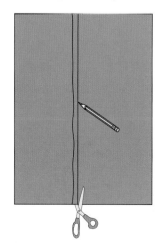

3. Turn the cut edge under and hand stitch it to the first section with an invisible binding stitch.

4. Repeat to join the remaining sections.

5. Trim and bind the quilt using your preferred method (see Finishing and Trimming, page 23).

Quarter Sections

Some quilts are easily divided into quarters. In this quilt as-you-go method, you will join the quarter sections together by stitching decorative sashing between them.

Note If you use the quarter method, keep in mind that the sections can be heavy, so you might need extra support around you to prevent drag, like extra tables around your sewing table.

The quarter method is used in the quilt project *You've Got a Friend* (page 76).

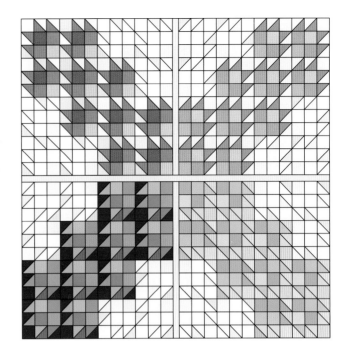

Quilting Quarter Sections

1. Layer the pieced quilt top, the batting, and the backing (see Layering Columnar Sections, page 13) and baste (see Basting Columnar Sections, page 13).

With this method, you can quilt right up to the edges of the sections because you're joining the sections with a sashing.

2. Trim the batting and the backing even with the pieced quilt top once the sandwich is quilted.

Joining Quarter Sections

Make sure the four sections of the quilt are the same dimensions.

Note The quilt doesn't have to be square. The sections can be rectangular. The sashings will run between the sections both horizontally and vertically. This method can also be used for a quilt with more than four sections.

1. Measure the vertical length of the quilted sandwich section along the edge that will be in the center of the quilt.

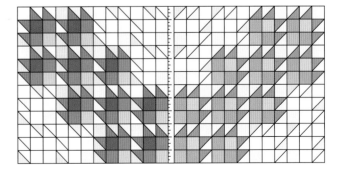

2. Cut a strip of fabric that coordinates with the quilt top. The strip should be 1½″ wide × the measurement from Step 1.

3. Cut another strip of fabric that coordinates with the backing fabric. This strip should be 1¼" wide × the measurement from Step 1.

4. Along the central edge, lay the 1½" strip on the quilt top and lay the 1¼" strip on the quilt back, right sides of each of the fabrics together, and pin securely or hand baste.

TIP

I suggest hand basting with a needle and thread—using a running stitch of about 3 stitches per inch—when attaching the strips to the quilt sandwich. Pins are acceptable, but you will get greater control with hand basting.

5. Using a walking foot and approximately 10 stitches per inch, stitch through all three layers: the quilt sandwich and the two sashings. Be sure that the sashing strip that is next to the feed dogs (underneath) remains flat.

6. Place the right side of the back of the next quilt sandwich section together with the right side of the back strip. Pin or hand baste securely.

Join the right side of the strip on the back to the quilt back.

Note Because these are scrap quilts, the backing fabric of one section of the quilt sandwich is different than the backing fabric of the first quilt sandwich section.

7. Stitch the back strip to the second quilt sandwich section, using a walking foot and approximately 10 stitches per inch.

8. Open the two quilt sandwiches to lie flat. Press the back sashing strip flat.

9. Press the front sashing strip toward Section 2.

10. Fold the raw edge of the front sashing strip under by ¼" and press.

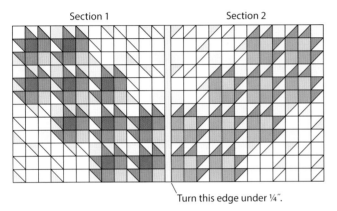

Section 1   Section 2

Turn this edge under ¼".

11. Pin the pressed edge down over Section 2.

12. Using a walking foot and approximately 10 stitches per inch, stitch the edge down along the fold.

13. Repeat to join Sections 3 and 4.

Note Joining the sections may also require rolling a large part of the quilt sandwich into the throat of the machine and feeding it through as you are stitching. Be aware that you will need a large table and support for the large roll. You will most likely have the roll in your lap (rather than hanging down).

Joining Half Sections

Once Sections 1 and 2 have been joined and Sections 3 and 4 have been joined, the two halves must be joined.

1. Measure the horizontal width of the joined sections along the edge that will in be the center of the quilt.

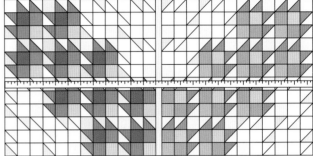

Note The measurement must equal the finished measurement of the block × the number of blocks + the finished measurement of the sashing in the center. This is the true measurement that the strip should be cut.

2. Cut a strip of fabric that coordinates with the quilt top. The strip should be 1½" wide × the measurement from Step 1.

3. Cut another strip of fabric that coordinates with the backing fabric. This strip should be 1¼" wide × the measurement from Step 1.

4. Repeat Steps 4–12 of Joining Quarter Sections (pages 18–19) for the long horizontal strips that join the upper and lower sections.

The four sections are now joined. You can also use this method to stitch a quilt as-you-go quilt that has more than four sections.

Sash-In-A-Dash

Photo courtesy of: Jill Repp of June Tailor, Inc.

Sash-In-A-Dash is a product invented and developed by Jill Repp of June Tailor, Inc. that allows quilt sections to be joined by encasing the raw unfinished edges of the quilt sandwich much like the quarter method.

Sash-In-A-Dash comes in multiple colors and can be purchased by the yard. If you can't find a color that matches your quilt, see Making Your Own Binding Sashing (below right) for instructions on how to make your own. I suggest you play around with Sash-In-A-Dash before attempting to make your own.

If you're using Sash-In-A-Dash, quilt all the way to the edges of the quilt sandwich. I would also recommend adding fabric around the quilt blocks, which will add space between the blocks and the Sash-In-A-Dash. Each side of Sash-In-A-Dash is 1" wide, so you may need the extra fabric to prevent cutting off any points on your blocks.

Sashings were added to the columns so that the points were not cut off by the Sash-In-A-Dash.

Make certain that your quilt sandwich pieces all have the same dimensions. Use a walking foot and a slightly longer stitch.

1. Cut the Sash-In-A-Dash to the exact length of the quilted pieces.

Note Sash-In-A-Dash acts like a casing. The edges of the quilted piece are inserted all the way into the center of the casing.

2. Insert the quilt sandwich section into the Sash-In-A-Dash so that the edges are completely encased and the sandwich is all the way into the center of the Sash-In-A-Dash.

3. Pin the edges securely.

4. Stitch close to the fold, making certain to catch all three layers: the Sash-In-A-Dash on the front, the quilt sandwich, and the Sash-In-A-Dash on the back.

TIP
You may need to stitch further in from the folded edge to catch the Sash-In-A-Dash on the back. Keep checking your work as you go to make certain you are catching all three layers.

Making Your Own Binding Sashing

Sash-In-A-Dash is a registered trade name, so I call this make-it-yourself version binding sashing. Binding sashing strips are cut on the straight grain instead of on the bias like Sash-In-A-Dash.

I recommend making a few short sections of binding sashing to get familiar with the stitching and pressing method. Once you feel comfortable, you can make full-length sections for your quilt all at once if you prefer.

Calculating Yardage

Calculate the lengths of the pieces that you will be using. Measure the blocks and rows or columns (or both) and multiply those measurements by the number of sashing pieces needed. This measurement will then be multiplied by 2 to make the double-wide binding sashing.

Here's an example for a quilt with 12″ × 12″ blocks in a 3 × 3 setting.

There will be 6 vertical binding sashing pieces between the blocks and 2 horizontal binding sashing pieces between the rows. The horizontal binding sashing pieces will be sewn onto the blocks after the blocks have been joined into rows with the vertical pieces.

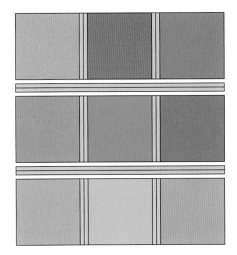

6 pieces of vertical binding sashing: 6 × 12″ = 72″

2 pieces of horizontal binding sashing: 2 × (3 × 12″) = 72″

Total length of pieces: 72″ + 72″ = 144″

Grand total length of binding strips to make binding sashing: 2 × 144″ = 288″

The binding sashing strips will be cut 4″ wide. Assuming you have 40″-wide fabric, divide the grand total length of binding sashing strips by 40″ to find how many fabric strips you will need. Round up to a full number of strips and add 1 extra for backup. Multiply the total number of strips by 4″ to get the total inches of fabric you will need. Divide this number by 36″ to convert the measurement to yards.

> In this example, the yardage would be calculated as follows:
>
> 288″ / 40″ = 7.2 strips
> (Round up to 8 and add 1 extra.)
>
> 9 strips × 4″ = 36″
>
> 36″ / 36″ = 1 yard

How it is Made

1. Cut the number of strips needed to make the grand total length of binding sashing (4″ × the width of fabric). Following the same example, this would be 288″, or 8 strips.

2. Join the strips, right sides together, to create 2 long strips. Piece the 4″ strips on the diagonal to reduce the bulk of the seams across all the folds and press the seam allowances.

3. Fold 1 strip in half lengthwise and press firmly.

4. Open the pressed strip and place it, right sides together, on top of the second strip, matching the edges. Sew together along the center fold.

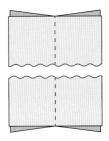

5. Press the strips closed, using the stitching line as a fold line.

6. Fold each long edge, wrong sides together, to the center seam and press, matching the upper and lower pressed edges.

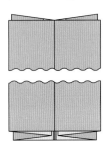

7. Follow Steps 1–4 of the instructions for Sash-In-A-Dash to sew the binding sashing between the blocks, rows, columns, or sections.

On-Point Quilts

I love to put quilt blocks on point. A quilt block can look completely different when it's on point as opposed to when it's just straight set. To quilt as-you-go when your blocks are on point, you join the diagonal rows in sections as you would with columns.

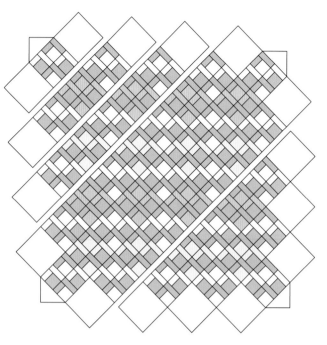

The sections will be joined after the blocks are quilted. When quilting, stay at least ½" from the edges that will be joined together, just as you would in the columnar method.

Finish the back exactly as you would in the columnar method (see Joining/Seaming Columnar Sections, page 14).

As a longtime sewist and quilter, I always use squares at the ends of my on-point rows instead of setting triangles. This can be viewed as wasteful, but as a scrap quilter, I save all my scraps and will eventually use them. Using squares at the end of the rows prevents distortion and wavy edges. I quilt right up to the edge and then trim them to the correct size just before binding. The advantage to doing it this way is that you can use the same size square that you used for all the other blocks. I do still use corner setting triangles for the four corners.

Finishing and Trimming

1. Lay the entire quilt onto a cutting surface where there is minimal to no drag on the quilt.

2. Place your quilting ruler ¼" away from the finished corner of the pieced blocks, across the solid squares.

3. Trim across all the layers of the quilt using your rotary cutter. There will be fabric and batting scraps, but this will keep the quilt from having wavy edges.

4. Bind the quilt using your preferred method very soon after trimming and avoid handling the edges.

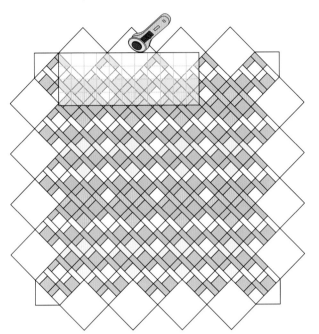

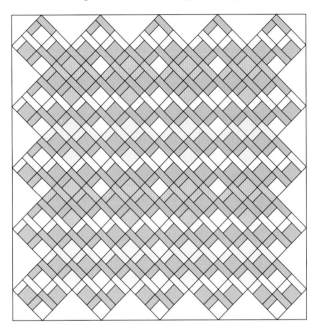

I hope that this demystifies the quilt as-you-go process. We shall forge ahead with color selection and specific projects.

Color Selection for Scrap Quilts

We've been hard at work concentrating on the quilt as-you-go methods, but this is still a book about scrap quilting, right? Some people are paralyzed by color selection for scrap quilting. I used to be among them and was a bit intimidated. Not anymore! I made up some rules for myself that haven't failed me yet, and I travel around the country and teach this method of color selection. I make it simple for myself and others.

First, gather your fabric scraps. All of my fabric scraps are separated into clear containers. If it's smaller than a fat quarter, it's a scrap. My scraps are typically larger than most quilter's scraps; I have scraps from bolt ends, scraps left over from garment sewing, and scraps from shop samples. I also save small scraps so long as they are larger than 3½″ square.

Next, grab a color wheel. Any color wheel is better than none, but I use the Essential Color Wheel Companion (C&T Publishing). I use this one because all the shades and tints are on it, and it's all in one place. I don't have to use pages or a flip chart—it's all right in front of me.

Finally, choose a color scheme. I have five simple schemes that I choose from every single time—my color decision tree. These are five color schemes that I use:

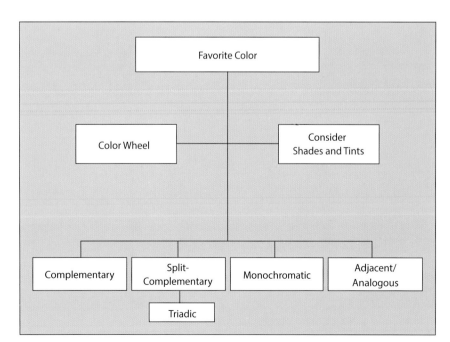

1. Monochromatic simply means all of one color. All shades and tints of one color can be included, but they must all be one color with a neutral. A *neutral* is a tan, gray, or white.

2. Complementary means that the colors are across from each other on the color wheel. For example, I will use blue and brown because brown is a shade of orange, and orange and blue are across from each other on the color wheel.

3. Triadic means a set of three colors that are indicated by drawing an equilateral triangle anywhere on the color wheel. Whichever colors are touched by the points of the triangle will be colors that will work well together.

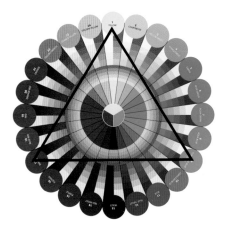

4. Adjacent (analogous) means colors that are right next to each other on the color wheel. This is my favorite color scheme and I use it the most! Two or three or as many as five or six adjacent colors can be used together with great effect.

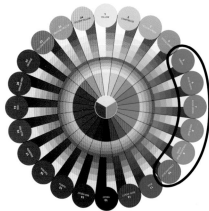

5. Split-complementary (complementary with adjacents) means adding the color directly across the color wheel from a grouping of adjacent colors. I love adjacent color schemes and use them a lot in my quilts—this color scheme is magic! People usually refer to this as a "pop" of color. They're never sure why it works, but it's because the color that pops is the opposite of the group of colors.

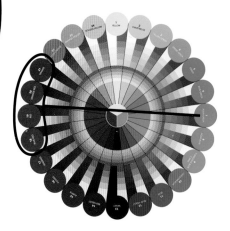

Fractured Four-Patch

The best part of all of this is that it's been determined by science. Someone else decided which colors on the color wheel look good together in various combinations. I just love to use this to my advantage and you can, too!

A great example of an adjacent color scheme can be found in this quilt from my book *Sensational Quilts for Scrap Lovers*.

In it, I used this section of the color wheel, including shades and tints. There are a few neutrals as well.

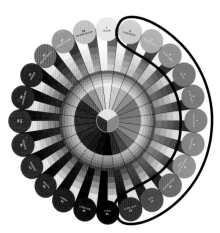

The Treasure Box Block

I used this block in several of the projects in this book; *Point Counterpoint* (page 34), *Mountains Majesty* (page 96), and *Tucson Sunset* (page 106).

I devised a quick-cut method that makes very short work of scraps using the fast2cut 3-in-1 Simple Square Template by C&T Publishing. (You can also easily rotary cut the shapes instead of using the template.) This works well because the scraps only need to be ironed and then you can set the template on top of each scrap and cut it out with a rotary cutter—kind of like a cookie cutter. If the scrap can accommodate a 5½″ square, it is large enough.

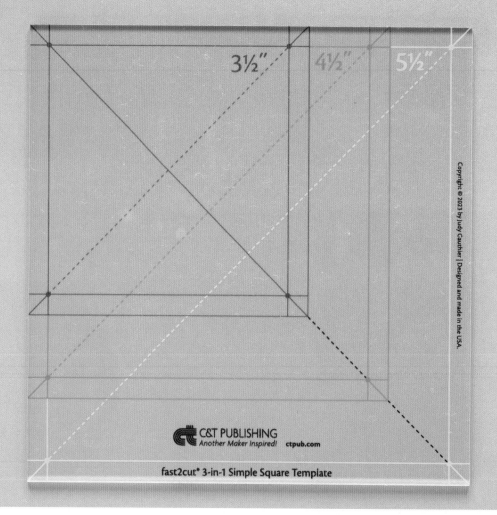

Note What about the bias edge? You may be trying to use a scrap of fabric that will only accommodate the 5½″ square template when it's not placed along the grain. If the square must be cut against (at an angle to) the grain, you will need to either be excruciatingly careful with that piece of fabric so that it doesn't stretch, or you will need to back it with a piece of lightweight interfacing.

STARCH DOESN'T PREVENT STRETCH

What I am about to say will send shock waves through the quilting community. *Do not rely on starch to keep something from stretching.* Starch does not prevent the fabric from stretching. It makes fabric stiff and it makes fabric flat after ironing, but it doesn't prevent stretching. It's not an astringent.

This is a piece of fabric cut on the bias. I sprayed it heavily with spray starch, let the starch soak in, and then ironed it. Then I stretched the bias edge with moderate handling.

This is the other side of the bias cut where no spray starch was applied and the same amount of stretch was applied to the piece.

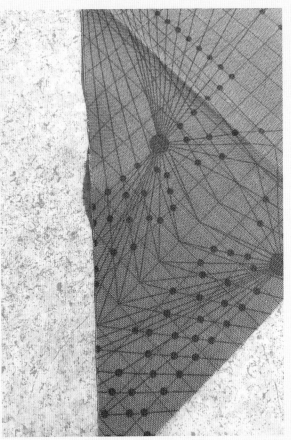

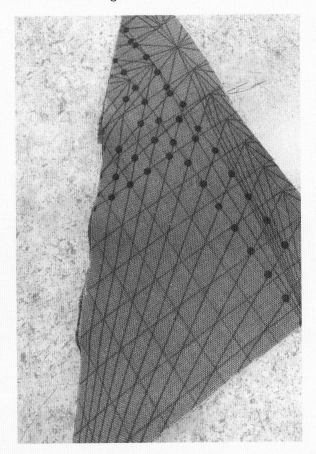

If it were true that starch prevented stretching, I would not have been able to distort this piece with moderate handling.

Cutting the Block

1. Cut 2 squares, 5½" × 5½" from your scraps. You can use the fast2cut 3-in-1 Simple Square Template or a ruler and rotary cutter.

2. Cut 2 contrasting squares, 5½" × 5½".

3. Stack them, making sure the edges are even.

4. Place the 3½" × 3½" template along the upper edge of the stack of squares, making sure that the 3½" marking line is on the left edge of the squares.

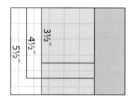

5. Cut along the edge of the template. This will yield a 2" × 5½" strip of fabric and the 3½" × 5½" strip.

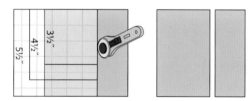

6. Make sure the 3½"-square mark on the ruler is positioned on the lower section of the wider strip. Cut across the top. This will yield a 3½" × 3½" square and a 2" × 3½" rectangle.

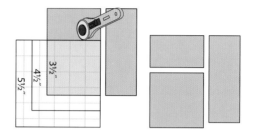

All the cutting for this fun block is done! Now to arrange the pieces.

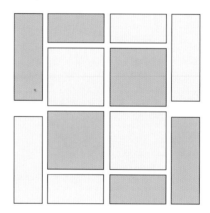

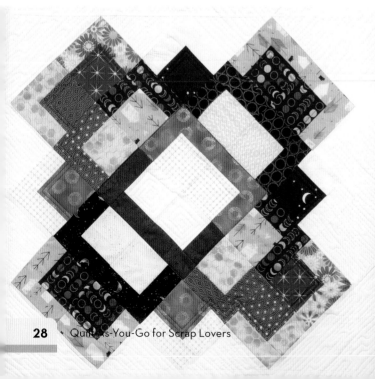

Stitching the Block

All seam allowances are ¼" wide and pressed open unless otherwise noted.

1. Stitch the 2" × 3½" rectangles of one fabric to the contrasting 3½" × 3½" squares, and vice versa.

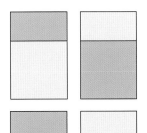

2. Press all seam allowances.

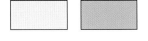

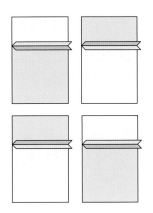

3. Stitch the 2" × 5½" rectangles along the edges of the units created in Steps 1 and 2 and press the seam allowances.

4. Trim the "tail" from the 2" × 5½" strip, leaving a 5" × 5" unit, or trim the unit to 4½" × 4½".

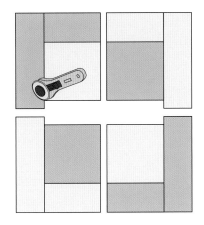

Note Some of the patterns using this method square the units to 4½" × 4½". Some of the patterns only trim the tail and then sew the units together as a four-patch.

5. Stitch the units together in an alternating four-patch to make the block.

6. Press the seam allowances.

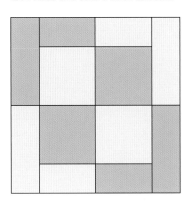

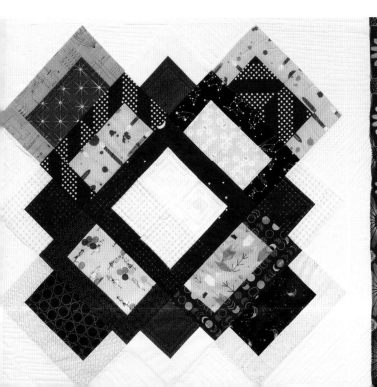

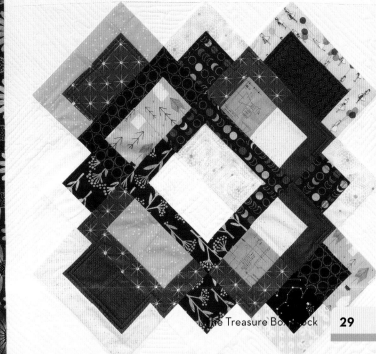

Pink Diamonds

FINISHED QUILT: 86" × 111½"

This is a monochromatic quilt. It's one color–pink–with neutrals. The neutrals are a mix of background-type fabrics. There are a good number of metallic fabrics as metallic fabrics are my passion. This quilt was done using horizontal columnar sections (see Columnar Sections, page 12).

Materials

Pink: 5 yards total of assorted scraps at least 5½″ × 5½″

Off-white: 5 yards total of assorted scraps at least 5½″ × 5½″

Batting: 3½ yards of 90″-wide

Backing: 8 yards

Binding: ⅞ yard

Cutting

Pink
Cut 216 squares 5½″ × 5½″.

Off-white
Cut 216 squares 5½″ × 5½″.

Batting
Cut 3 rectangles 39″ × 88″.

Backing
Cut 3 rectangles 92″ × width of fabric.

Binding
Cut 11 strips 2½″ × width of fabric.

Make the Triangle Units

All seam allowances are ¼″ wide and pressed open, unless otherwise noted.

Pink Triangles

1. Stitch 2 pink squares, right sides together, along one edge.

2. Open and press the seam allowances.

3. Repeat with a second pair of pink squares.

4. Place the 2 pairs of squares, right sides together and seams matching.

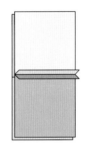

5. Stitch along the long edge of both sides of the pair.

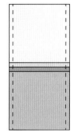

6. Place a quilting ruler diagonally from the upper left corner of the pairs to the lower right corner.

7. Cut along the ruler with a rotary cutter.

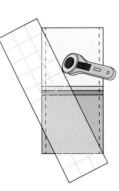

8. Open the triangles and press the seam allowances.

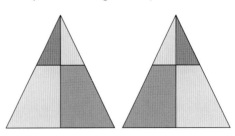

9. Repeat to make 108 pink triangles.

Off-White Triangles

Repeat Steps 1–8 of Pink Triangles (page 31) to make 96 off-white triangles.

Off-White Half Triangles

1. Repeat Steps 1–4 of Pink Triangles with pairs of off-white squares. Do not stitch along the long edges.

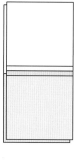

2. Place a quilting ruler diagonally from the upper left corner to the lower right corner.

3. Cut along the ruler with a rotary cutter.

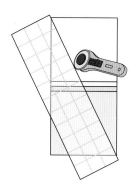

4. Repeat Steps 1–3 to yield 24 half triangles.

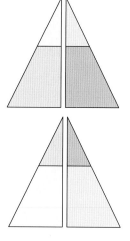

Assemble the Sections

First Row

The triangle rows are created by inverting every other triangle to create a straight row (see the quilt photo, page 30).

1. Place an off-white half triangle, right sides together, along the left side of a pink triangle. The wide base of the pink triangle will line up with the tip of the off-white triangle.

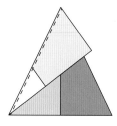

Note The center horizontal seams of the triangles will not line up.

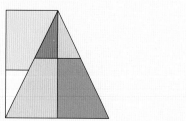

2. Stitch the seam and press the seam allowance.

3. Place an off-white triangle, right sides together, along the right side of the first pink triangle.

4. Stitch and press the seam allowance.

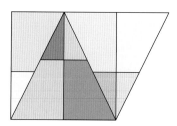

5. Repeat until there are 9 pink triangles, 8 off-white triangles, and off-white half triangles at each end. The half triangles will be mirror images of each other.

Second Row

Note The second row is a mirror image of the first row.

1. Place an off-white half triangle, right sides together, with a pink triangle. The pink triangle is inverted and the half triangle will have the point facing up.

2. Stitch and press the seam allowances.

3. Place an off-white full triangle, right sides together, on the right-hand side with the pink triangle.

4. Stitch and press the seam allowances.

5. Repeat Steps 1–4 until there are 9 pink triangles and 8 off-white triangles with the half-triangles at both ends.

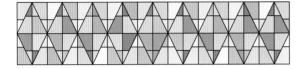

6. Stitch the second row to the first row, right sides together and matching the center seams of the pink triangles and the points of the off-white triangles. Press the seam allowances.

Put 4 Rows Together for a Section

1. Repeat First Row, Steps 1–5 (page 32).

2. Repeat Second Row Steps 1–6 (left).

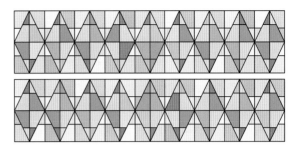

3. Stitch the second section of 2 rows to the first section of 2 rows with right sides together, matching the points of the pink triangles and the center seams of the off-white triangles.

4. Press all seam allowances. It should measure 37″ × 86″.

5. Repeat Steps 1–4 to create two more sections.

Quilt As-You-Go

1. Layer each section with batting and backing and baste (see Layering Columnar Sections, page 13, and Basting Columnar Sections, page 13).

2. Quilt in columnar fashion (see Quilting Columnar Sections, page 14).

3. Trim away any excess fabric from the edges of the quilt.

4. Join the sections (see Joining/Seaming Columnar Sections, page 14).

5. Trim away any excess fabric from the edges of the quilt (see Finishing and Trimming, page 23).

6. Bind your quilt using your preferred method.

Quilt assembly

Point Counterpoint

FINISHED BLOCK: 16" × 16" ◆ **FINISHED QUILT:** 80½" × 80½"

The best part about this quilt is that it looks like it's an on-point set. The blocks have that look but they're a straight set, which makes it easier to quilt as-you-go, and there are no setting triangles. I call that a victory!

This is based on The Treasure Box Block (page 26), which is prevalent in my previous scrap quilting books. It's such a versatile block—there are hundreds of possible layouts!

This quilt has an adjacent (analogous) color scheme. The colors used are shown to the right on the color wheel.

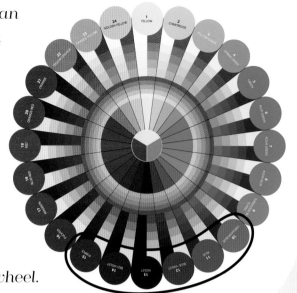

Materials

Colored print: 4¾ yards total of assorted scraps at least 5½″ × 5½″

White: 4¾ yards

Batting: 2¾ yards of 90″-wide

Backing: 7½ yards

Binding: ¾ yard

Cutting

Colored print
Cut 200 squares 5½″ × 5½″.

White
Cut 29 strips 5½″ × width of fabric.

  Subcut 200 squares 5½″ × 5½″.

Batting
Cut 5 rectangles 19″ × 83″.

Backing
Cut 5 rectangles 20″ × 87″.

Binding
Cut 9 strips 2½″ × width of fabric.

Note I pieced the back with multiple different fabrics. Quilt as-you-go is advantageous in that you can use fabrics from your stash for the backing. Because you are making the quilt in sections, you can use a different fabric for each section.

Make the Blocks

All seam allowances are ¼″ wide and pressed open unless otherwise noted.

Making the Treasure Box Units

There are two ways that you can measure to cut the pieces for this block. You can use the fast2cut 3-in-1 Simple Square Template, or you can use a conventional ruler. The stack and cut method can be found in The Treasure Box Block, Cutting the Block (page 28). Both ways will be discussed.

Stack and Cut Method

1. Stack 2 printed squares 5½″ × 5½″ with 2 white squares 5½″ × 5½″, making certain that all edges are even.

2. Cut using the stack and cut method for The Treasure Box Block, Cutting the Block, Steps 3–6 (page 28).

Conventional Ruler Cutting Method

1. Stack 2 printed squares 5½" × 5½" with 2 white squares 5½" × 5½", making certain that all edges are even.

2. Using a quilting ruler, cut a 2" × 5½" strip from the left side of the squares.

3. From the remaining stack of 3½" × 5½" rectangles, cut a 3½" × 3½" square using a quilting ruler.

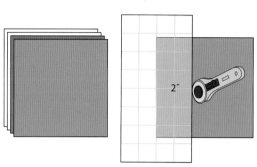

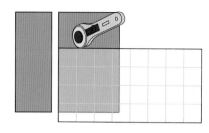

Stitching the Treasure Box Units for Both Methods

1. Stitch the white squares and print rectangles together following The Treasure Box Block, Stitching the Block, Steps 1–3 of (page 29).

2. Trim the units to 4½" × 4½" using a 4½" template or a fast2cut 3-in-1 Simple Square Template by C&T Publishing.

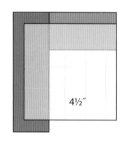

Note When trimming the units to 4½" × 4½", be sure that the entire square is left untrimmed, but the rectangles are trimmed.

3. Repeat The Treasure Box Block, Stitching the Block, Steps 1–3 (page 29) with the print squares and white rectangles to finish 2 components for the large block.

Making the Half-Square Triangles

1. Stack a white square, right sides together, with a print square.

2. Draw a diagonal line from one corner to the opposite corner on the white square.

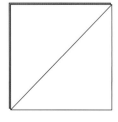

3. Stitch ¼" on both sides of the line.

4. Cut on the line.

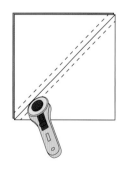

5. Open and press the seam allowances.

6. This yields 2 half-square triangle units.

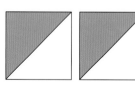

7. Trim the half-square triangle units to 4½" × 4½", making certain that the diagonal line on the template is

positioned on top of the seam.

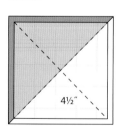

8. Repeat Steps 1–7 to create a total of 8 half-square-triangle units per block.

Combine the Units

1. Arrange the units to create the block.

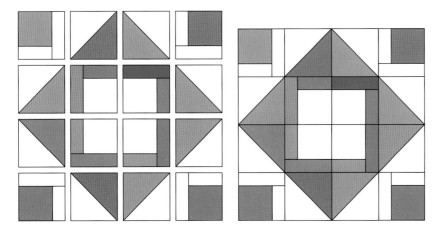

2. Stitch the units, right sides together, into rows, paying attention to the orientation of the squares.

3. Press all the seam allowances.

4. With right sides together and matching seams, stitch the rows together to make a block.

5. Open and press the seams.

Combine the Blocks into Rows

1. Arrange a row of 5 blocks.

2. With right sides together and matching seams, stitch the blocks together.

3. Press the seam allowances.

4. Repeat Steps 1–3 to make 5 rows. Refer to the quilt assembly diagram (below).

Quilt As-You-Go

1. Layer each row with batting and backing and baste (see Layering Columnar Sections, page 13, and Basting Columnar Sections, page 13).

2. Quilt in columnar fashion (see Quilting Columnar Sections, page 14).

3. Trim away any excess fabric from the edges of the quilt.

4. Join the sections (see Joining/Seaming Columnar Sections, page 14).

5. Trim away any excess fabric from the edges of the quilt (see Finishing and Trimming, page 23).

6. Bind the quilt using your preferred method.

Quilt assembly

Interweave

FINISHED QUILT: 82½″ × 82½″

Quilt As-You-Go for Scrap Lovers

This quilt is a true scrap challenge. The strips change prints while the color remains the same. The challenge here is to look through your scraps and find colors that have different prints but are the same color. There is movement along the strips and if it is done well, the change in prints won't be obvious until the viewer moves in to take a closer look. I teach a class on how to do this skillfully in any quilt. This is great practice.

The background blocks are gray. My favorite gray to use as a neutral is Moda Fabrics Zen Gray. This gray does not lean blue or brown. It can be hard to find a gray that is just white mixed with black and this cinches it.

Materials

Use a variety of scraps at least the sizes noted in the cutting list.

Jade: 7/8 yard total of assorted scraps

Turquoise: 3/4 yard total of assorted scraps

Royal: 1¼ yards total of assorted scraps

Red: ½ yard total of assorted scraps

Violet: 5/8 yard total of assorted scraps

Red-Orange: 3/4 yard total of assorted scraps

Gold: 1½ yards total of assorted scraps

Orange: 3/4 yard total of assorted scraps

Green: 1¼ yards total of assorted scraps

Hot Pink: ½ yard total of assorted scraps

Navy: 3/8 yard total of assorted scraps

Gray: 1¾ yards

Batting: 1 square 90″ × 90″

Backing: 7¾ yards

Binding: 3/4 yard

Cutting

Jade
Cut 12 strips 2½″ × 5½″.
Cut 12 strips 2½″ × 11½″.
Cut 4 strips 2½″ × 16½″.

Turquoise
Cut 20 strips 2½″ × 5½″.
Cut 12 strips 2½″ × 11½″.

Royal
Cut 12 strips 2½″ × 5½″.
Cut 12 strips 2½″ × 11½″.
Cut 12 strips 2½″ × 16½″.

Red
Cut 10 strips 2½″ × 5½″.
Cut 6 strips 2½″ × 11½″.

Violet
Cut 3 strips 2½″ × 5½″.
Cut 3 strips 2½″ × 11½″.
Cut 5 strips 2½″ × 16½″.

Red Orange
Cut 20 strips 2½″ × 5½″.
Cut 12 strips 2½″ × 11½″.

Gold
Cut 40 strips 2½″ × 5½″.
Cut 24 strips 2½″ × 11½″.

Orange
Cut 9 strips 2½″ × 5½″.
Cut 9 strips 2½″ × 11½″.
Cut 3 strips 2½″ × 16½″.

Green
Cut 18 strips 2½″ × 5½″.
Cut 18 strips 2½″ × 11½″.
Cut 6 strips 2½″ × 16½″.

Hot Pink
Cut 10 strips 2½″ × 5½″.
Cut 6 strips 2½″ × 11½″.

Navy
Cut 5 strips 2½″ × 5½″.
Cut 3 strips 2½″ × 11½″.

Gray
Cut 64 squares 5½″ × 5½″.

Batting
Cut 1 rectangle 36″ × 85″.
Cut 1 rectangle 52″ × 85″.

Backing
Cut 3 rectangles 89″ × width of fabric.
  Subcut 1 rectangle in half lengthwise to be 20″ × 89″.

Binding
Cut 9 strips 2½″ × width of fabric.

Make the Quilt Top

All seam allowances are ¼" wide and pressed open unless otherwise noted.

> **Note** This quilt could be put together in a dozen different ways. When I first wrote the pattern, it was a complex process to get the over and under effect. Any experienced quilter could most likely find their own way of putting the units together. I want to provide the basic fabric requirements and placement so that you can enjoy the process.

Make the Components

Gold and Red-Orange Units

1. With right sides together, stitch a gold 2½" × 5½" strip to a red-orange 2½" × 5½" strip.

2. With right sides together, stitch a second gold 2½" × 5½" strip to the opposite side of the Red strip.

3. Repeat Steps 1 and 2 to make 20 units. Label them GR1.

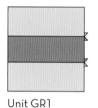

Unit GR1

4. With right sides together, stitch a gray 5½" × 5½" square to a gold side of unit GR1.

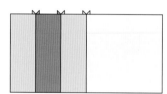

5. With right sides together, stitch a second gray 5½" × 5½" square to the opposite side of unit GR1.

6. Repeat Steps 1–5 to make 20 units and label them GRG.

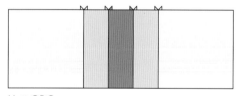

Unit GRG

7. With right sides together, stitch a gold 2½" × 11½" strip to a red-orange 2½" × 11½" strip.

8. With right sides together, stitch a second gold 2½" × 11½" strip to the opposite side of the red-orange strip.

9. Repeat Steps 7 and 8 to make 12 units and label them GRO.

Jade and Royal Units

1. With right sides together, stitch a jade 2½″ × 11½″ strip to a royal 2½″ × 11½″ strip.

2. With right sides together, stitch another jade 2½″ × 11½″ strip to the opposite side of the royal strip. Press the seam allowances.

3. Repeat Steps 1 and 2 to make 6 units. Label them JRJ.

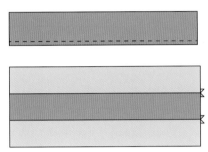

Unit JRJ

4. With right sides together, stitch a jade 2½″ × 5½″ strip to a royal 2½″ × 5½″ strip.

5. With right sides together, stitch a second jade 2½″ × 5½″ strip to the opposite side of the royal strip.

6. Repeat Steps 4 and 5 to make 6 units. Label them JRJ Short.

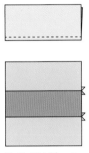

Unit JRJ Short

7. With right sides together, stitch a jade 2½″ × 16½″ strip to a royal 2½″ × 16½″ strip.

8. With right sides together, stitch a second jade 2½″ × 16½″ strip to the other side of the royal strip. Make 2 units Label them JRJ Long.

Unit JRJ Long

Green and Orange Units

1. With right sides together, stitch a green 2½″ × 5½″ strip to an orange 2½″ × 5½″ strip.

2. With right sides together, stitch a second green 2½″ × 5½″ strip to the opposite side of the orange strip. Press the seam allowances.

3. Repeat Steps 1 and 2 to make 9 units. Label them GOG Short.

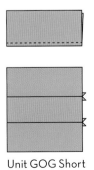

Unit GOG Short

4. Repeat Steps 1 and 2 using green and orange 2½″ × 11½″ strips to make 9 units. Label them GOG.

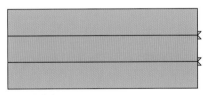

Unit GOG

5. Repeat Steps 1 and 2 using green and orange 2½″ × 16½″ strips and make 3 units. Label them GOG Long.

Unit GOG Long

Turquoise and Red Units

1. With right sides together, stitch a turquoise 2½″ × 5½″ strip to a red 2½″ × 5½″ strip.

2. With right sides together, stitch a second turquoise 2½″ × 5½″ strip to the opposite side of the red strip.

3. Repeat Steps 1 and 2 to make 10 units. Label them TRT Short.

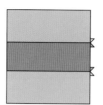

Unit TRT Short

4. Repeat Steps 1 and 2 using turquoise and red 2½″ × 11½″ strips to make 6 units. Label them TRT.

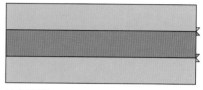

Unit TRT

Royal and Violet Units

1. With right sides together, stitch a royal 2½″ × 5½″ strip to a violet 2½″ × 5½″ strip.

2. With right sides together, stitch a second royal 2½″ × 5½″ strip to the opposite side of the violet strip.

3. Repeat to make 3 units. Label them RVR Short.

Unit RVR Short

4. Repeat Steps 1 and 2 using royal and violet 2½″ × 11½″ strips to make 3 units. Label them RVR.

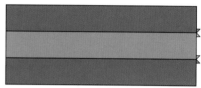

Unit RVR

5. Repeat Steps 1 and 2 using royal and violet 2½″ × 16½″ strips to make 5 units. Label them RVR Long.

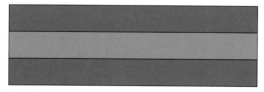

Unit RVR Long

Hot Pink and Navy Units

1. With right sides together, stitch a hot pink 2½″ × 5½″ strip to a navy 2½″ × 5½″ strip.

2. With right sides together, stitch a second hot pink 2½″ × 5½″ strip to the opposite side of the navy strip.

3. Repeat Steps 1 and 2 to make 5 units. Label them PNP Short.

4. Repeat Steps 1 and 2 using hot pink and navy 2½″ × 11½″ strips to make 3 units. Label them PNP.

Make the Blocks

Unit 1

1. With right sides together, stitch a JRJ Short unit to a JRJ unit.

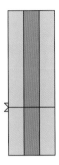

2. With right sides together, stitch a GRG unit to the unit from Step 1 along the left side of the unit from Step 1. Note the orientation.

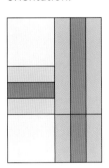

3. With right sides together, stitch a GOG unit to the bottom of the unit from Step 2. Note the orientation.

4. Repeat Steps 1–3 to create 6 units. Label them Unit 1.

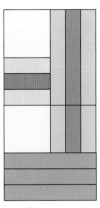

Unit 1

Unit 2

1. With right sides together, stitch a GRG unit to a JRJ Long unit. Note the orientation.

2. Make 2 units. Label them Unit 2.

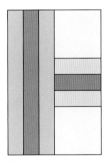

Unit 2

Unit 3

1. With right sides together, stitch a gray 5½″ × 5½″ square to the turquoise side of a TRT Short unit.

2. With right sides together, stitch a GRO unit to the unit from Step 1. Note the orientation.

3. Make 6 of these units. Label them Unit 3A.

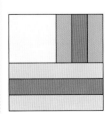

Unit 3A

4. With right sides together, stitch a gray 5½″ × 5½″ square to the green side of a GOG Short unit.

5. With right sides together, stitch a TRT unit to the unit from Step 4. Note the orientation.

6. Repeat to make 6 units. Label them Unit 3B.

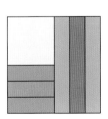

Unit 3B

7. With right sides together, stitch together units 3A and 3B. Note the orientation.

8. Repeat to make 6 units. Label them Unit 3.

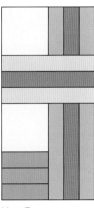

Unit 3

Unit 3+

1. Stitch a gray 5½" × 5½" square to the turquoise side of a TRT Short unit.

2. Repeat to make 4.

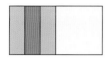

3. Stitch a GRO unit between 2 of the units created in Steps 1 and 2.

4. Repeat Step 3 to make 2 units. Label them Unit 3+.

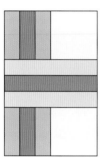

Unit 3+

Unit 4

1. With right sides together, stitch an RVR unit to an RVR Short unit.

2. Stitch a GRG unit to the left side of the unit from Step 1.

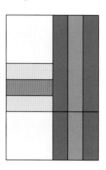

3. Stitch a GOG unit to the lower edge of the unit from Step 2.

4. Repeat Steps 1–3 to make 3 units. Label them Unit 4.

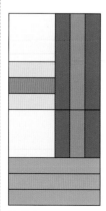

Unit 4

Unit 4+

1. Stitch a GRG unit to an RVR Long unit.

2. Label it Unit 4+.

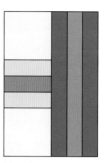

Unit 4+

Unit 5

1. Stitch a gray 5½" × 5½" square to a pink edge of a PNP Short unit. Note the orientation.

2. Stitch a GRO unit to the unit from Step 1.

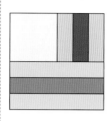

3. Stitch a 5½" × 5½" gray square to a GOG Short unit.

4. Stitch a PNP unit to the unit from Step 3.

5. Stitch the units from Steps 2 and 4 together. Note the orientation.

6. Repeat Steps 1–5 to make 3 units. Label them Unit 5.

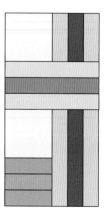

Unit 5

Unit 5+

1. Stitch a gray 5½" × 5½" square to a pink edge of a PNP Short unit. Note the orientation.

2. Repeat Step 1 to make 2 units.

3. Stitch a GRO unit to a unit from Step 1.

4. Stitch the second unit from Step 1 to the opposite side of the unit from Step 3. Label it Unit 5+.

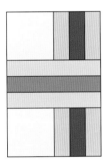

Unit 5+

Unit 6

1. With right sides together, stitch a GRG unit to an RVR Long unit.

2. Stitch a second GRG unit to the opposite side of the GRG unit from Step 1.

3. Stitch a GOG Long unit to the edge perpendicular to RVR Long unit.

4. Repeat Steps 1–3 to make 3 units. Label them Unit 6.

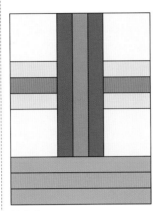

Unit 6

Unit 6+

Repeat Unit 6, Steps 1 and 2. Label it Unit 6+.

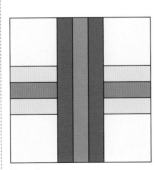

Unit 6+

Make the Columns

All units are stitched with right sides together and all seam allowances are pressed open.

Note It's more important to line up the seams on this quilt than on any of the others. The impression of complete strips (made from multiple smaller scraps) is what makes this quilt sing. It's important to make it look continuous.

Column 1

1. Stitch together 3 Units 1 into a column.

2. Stitch a Unit 2 to the end of the column.

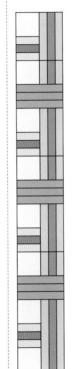

Column 2

1. Stitch together 3 Units 3 into a column.

2. Stitch a Unit 3+ to the end of the column.

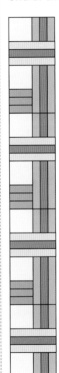

Column 3

1. Stitch together 3 Units 4 into a column.

2. Stitch a Unit 4+ to the end of the column.

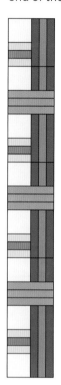

Column 4

1. Stitch together 3 Units 5 into a column.

2. Stitch a Unit 5+ to the end of the column.

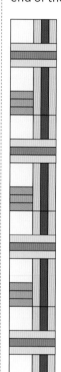

Column 5

1. Stitch together 3 Units 6 into a column.

2. Stitch a Unit 6+ to the end of the column.

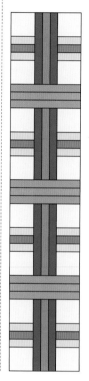

Column 6

Note Column 6 is identical to Column 2 except that the orientation is different (see the quilt assembly diagram). Column 6 is rotated 180°.

1. Stitch together 3 Units 3 into a column.

2. Stitch a Unit 3+ to the top of the column.

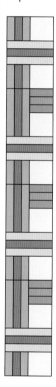

Column 7

Note Column 7 is identical to Column 1 except that the orientation is different (see the quilt assembly diagram). Column 7 is rotated 180°.

1. Stitch together 3 Units 1 into a column.

2. Stitch a Unit 2 to the top of the column.

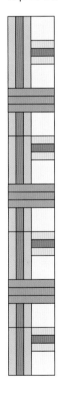

Sectioning for Quilt As-You-Go

Note This quilt uses the columnar method for quilt as-you-go (see Columnar Sections, page 12).

1. Stitch Column 1 to Column 2, right sides together and seams matching.

2. Open and press the seam allowances.

3. Stitch Column 3 to Column 2, right sides together and seams matching.

4. Open and press the seam allowances and set it aside.

5. Stitch Columns 4, 5, 6, and 7 with right sides together and seams matching.

6. Open and press the seam allowances.

Quilt As-You-Go

1. Layer a full width-of-fabric backing rectangle and the 36″ × 85″ batting rectangle with the quilt top section of Columns 1–3.

2. Baste.

3. With right sides together, stitch an full-width backing rectangle and a 20″ × 89″ backing rectangle together along the selvage edge using a ⅝″ seam allowance.

4. Press the seam allowances and press the entire backing piece.

5. Repeat Steps 1–2 for the backing section from Step 4 and the 52″ × 85″ batting rectangle with the remaining quilt top section of Columns 4–7.

6. Quilt in columnar fashion (see Quilting Columnar Sections, page 14).

7. Join the sections (see Joining/Seaming Columnar Sections, page 14).

8. Trim away any excess fabric from the edges of the quilt (see Finishing and Trimming, page 23).

9. Bind the quilt using your preferred method.

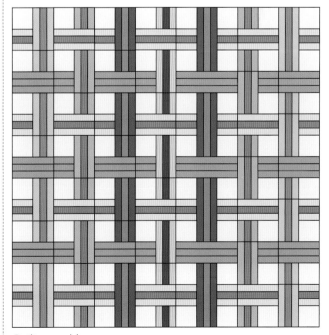

Quilt assembly

Rainy Days and Scrap Quilts

FINISHED QUILT: 78½" × 91½"

This quilt has a monochromatic color scheme. I simply tore into my blue scraps. Of course, there are a few pieces that needed to be slightly bigger than my scraps would accommodate so it allowed me to create more scraps from my fat quarters. There's one way to approach scrap quilting … make more scraps!

Sewing curves can be somewhat scary for some folks. After you finish this quilt, you will be a pro. I have a foolproof method for sewing curves that I call my manhole cover method. Have you ever watched someone put a manhole cover back onto a manhole? They roll the cover onto the opening around the edges. That's exactly how these curves are sewn. You will never look at curves the same way again.

Materials

Dark gray: ½ yard total of assorted scraps at least the size of the shapes to the right

Gray: 7 fat quarters of assorted gray prints

White and light gray: 10 fat quarters of assorted background-style fabrics

Dark blue: 3 yards of assorted scraps at least the size of the shapes shown (page 50)

Medium blue: 2 yards of assorted scraps at least the size of the shapes shown (page 50)

Light blue: 1¾ yards of assorted scraps at least the size of the shapes shown (page 50)

Batting: 2⅞ yards of 90"-wide

Backing: 7¼ yards

Binding: ⅞ yard

Cutting

Patterns for the clouds and raindrops are on pages 59–75.

Dark gray
Cut 1 of Under Cloud 1 and 1 reversed.

Cut 1 of Under Cloud 2 and 1 reversed.

Cut 1 of Upper Cloud 2 and 1 reversed.

Cut 1 of Upper Cloud 3 and 1 reversed.

Gray
Cut 1 of Cloud 1 and 1 reversed.

Cut 1 of Cloud 2 and 1 reversed.

Cut 1 of Cloud 3 and 1 reversed.

Cut 1 of Center Cloud.

Cutting continued on next page

White and light gray

Note The raindrops can be made of assorted scraps within each raindrop or with the same fabric in each raindrop.

Cut 18 of Raindrop Piece 1.

Cut 18 of Raindrop Piece 3.

Cut 18 of Raindrop Piece 6 and 18 reversed.

Dark blue

Cut 1 of Cloud Setting 1 and 1 reversed.

Cut 1 of Cloud Setting 2 and 1 reversed.

Cut 1 of Cloud Setting 3 and 1 reversed.

Cut 1 of Cloud Setting Center.

Cut 4 of Raindrop Piece 2 and 4 reversed.

Cut 4 of Raindrop Piece 5 and 4 reversed.

Cut 4 of Raindrop Piece 4.

Cut 4 squares 7½" × 7½".
Cut 136 squares 3½" × 3½".

Medium blue

Cut 7 of Raindrop Piece 2 and 7 reversed.

Cut 7 of Raindrop Piece 5 and 7 reversed.

Cut 7 of Raindrop Piece 4.

Cut 2 squares 7½" × 7½".
Cut 1 square 6½" × 6½".
Cut 123 squares 3½" × 3½".

Light blue

Cut 7 of Raindrop Piece 2 and 7 reversed.

Cut 7 of Raindrop Piece 5 and 7 reversed.

Cut 7 of Raindrop Piece 4.

Cut 1 of Center Cloud Under.

Cut 2 squares 7½" × 7½".
Cut 75 squares 3½" × 3½".

Batting

Cut 2 rectangles 32" × 81". Label them Section 1 and Section 2.
Cut 1 rectangle 18" × 81". Label it Section 3.
Cut 1 rectangle 17" × 81". Label it Cloud.

Backing

Cut 2 rectangles 36" × 85". Label them Section 1 and Section 2.
Cut 1 rectangle 85" × width of fabric.

   Subcut 2 rectangles 20" × 85". Label them Section 3 and Cloud.

Binding

Cut 10 strips 2½" × width of fabric.

SEWING CURVES

Align the center points of both pieces.

With the convex piece on top, pin at the aligned center points.

Pin at the aligned top corners.

Place a pin between the first 2 pins.

Add pins at the aligned bottom corners and between these pins and the center pins.

Stitch the curve, being careful not to stretch or pull the pieces. Press the seam allowances toward the convex curve.

Make the Cloud Blocks

All seam allowances are ¼" wide and pressed open unless otherwise noted. Refer to Sewing Curves (left).

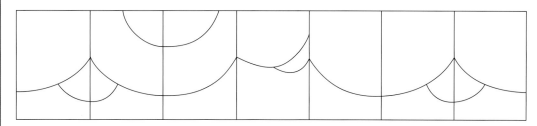

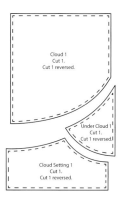

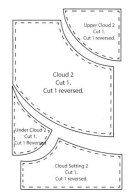

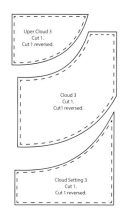

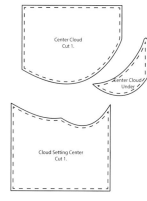

Cloud 1 and Cloud 1 Reversed

1. With right sides together, stitch the curved edge of Under Cloud 1 to the curved edge of Cloud Setting 1.

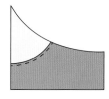

2. Stitch the curved edge of Cloud 1 to the curved edge of the Under Cloud 1 + Cloud Setting 1.

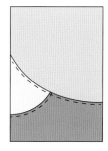

3. Press the seam allowances toward the convex curves.

4. Repeat Steps 1–3 for the reverse pieces of Under Cloud 1, Cloud Setting 1, and Cloud 1.

Cloud 2 and Cloud 2 Reversed

1. Stitch Under Cloud 2 to Cloud Setting 2.

2. Stitch Upper Cloud 2 to Cloud 2.

3. Stitch Cloud 2 to Under Cloud 2 + Cloud Setting 2 unit.

4. Press the seam allowances toward the convex curves.

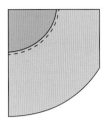

5. Repeat Steps 1–4 for the reverse pieces of Under Cloud 2, Cloud Setting 2, Upper Cloud 2, and Cloud 2.

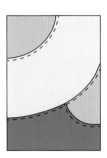

Cloud 3 and Cloud 3 Reversed

1. Stitch Cloud 3 to Cloud Setting 3.

2. Stitch Upper Cloud 3 to Cloud 3.

3. Press all seam allowances toward the convex curved pieces.

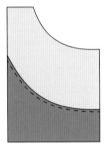

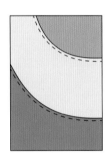

4. Repeat Steps 1–3 for reverse pieces of Cloud 3, Cloud Setting 3, and Upper Cloud 3.

Center Cloud

1. Stitch Center Cloud Under to Cloud Setting Center.

2. Stitch Center Cloud to the Center Cloud Under + Cloud Setting Center unit.

3. Press the seam allowances toward the convex curved pieces.

TIP..

Matching Seam Allowances on Curved Piecing

It can be tricky to match the seam allowances when there are curves Find the edges of the fabrics by looking between the pieces of fabric and placing a pin exactly where they intersect. Pin it securely. Insert a second pin to hold the corners together. Feel the junction with your fingers as you are sewing and make sure that your needle comes down exactly where they join.

Make the Cloud Row

1. Stitch Cloud 1 unit to Cloud 2 unit, matching the seams. Press the seam allowances.

2. Stitch Cloud 3 unit to Center Cloud, matching the seams. Press the seam allowances.

3. Stitch Cloud 3 Reversed unit to Cloud 2 Reversed unit, matching the seams. Press the seam allowances.

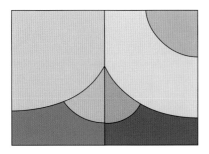 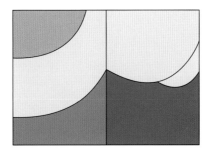 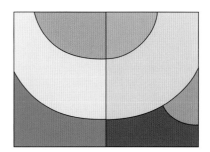

4. Stitch the cloud pairs from Steps 1–3 and Cloud 1 Reversed together to complete the cloud row. Press the seam allowances.

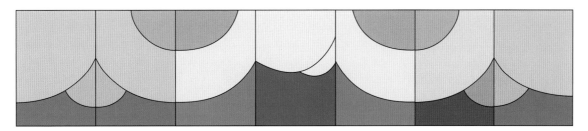

Make the Raindrop Blocks

1. With right sides together, stitch Raindrop Piece 2 to Raindrop Piece 1. Press the seam allowances.

2. With right sides together, stitch Raindrop Piece 2 Reversed to Raindrop Piece 1. Press the seam allowances.

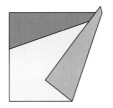

3. With right sides together, stitch Raindrop Piece 5 to Raindrop Piece 6. Press the seam allowances toward the convex Rainbow Piece 6.

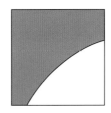

4. With right sides together, stitch Raindrop Piece 5 Reversed to Raindrop Piece 6 Reversed. Press the seam allowances toward the convex Rainbow Piece 6 Reversed.

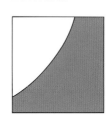

5. Stitch Raindrop Piece 3 to Raindrop Piece 4. Press the seam allowances toward the convex Rainbow Piece 3.

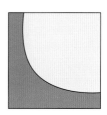

Sew the Combined Pieces Together

1. Stitch the Raindrop 5+6 to the unit Raindrop 2+1. Press the seam allowances.

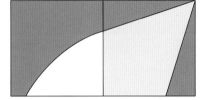

2. Stitch the Raindrop Combination Piece 3+4 from Make the Raindrop Blocks, Step 5 (page 53) to the Raindrop 5R+6R. Press the seam allowances.

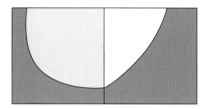

3. Stitch the 2 sections from Steps 1 and 2 together matching the center seam. Press the seam allowances.

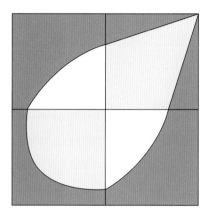

4. Repeat Steps 1–3 to make 18 raindrops.

Half-Square Triangle Units

1. With right sides together, stack 2 dark blue 7½″ × 7½″ squares.

2. Draw a diagonal line across the top square from one corner to the opposite corner.

3. Stitch ¼″ on both sides of the diagonal line.

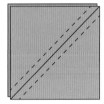

4. Cut on the diagonal line.

5. Open and press the seam allowances. This creates 2 dark blue half-square triangle units.

6. Repeat Steps 1–5 with the second pair of dark blue 7½″ × 7½″ squares.

7. Repeat Steps 1–5 with a pair of medium blue 7½″ × 7½″ squares and a pair of light blue 7½″ × 7½″ squares. There will be 1 extra light blue half-square triangle unit left over and 1 extra medium blue half-square triangle unit left over.

8. Trim the 4 dark blue, 1 medium, and 1 light blue half-square triangle units down to 6½″ × 6½″.

6½″ × 6½″

Note You can use the leftover half-square triangle units from Step 7 in place of 4 squares 3½″ × 3½″ in any place in the quilt if you wish. Trim the extra half-square triangle units to 6½″ × 6½″ to use them in the quilt.

3½"-Square Rows

1. With right sides together stitch a dark blue 3½" × 3½" square to another dark blue 3½" × 3½" square. Press the seam allowances.

2. Continue to stitch dark blue 3½" × 3½" squares to this row to make a row with 26 dark blue squares.

3. Repeat Steps 1 and 2 to make a second row of 26 dark blue squares.

Note You will be making multiple rows of 3½" squares. It adds interest to the quilt to occasionally use a dark blue square in a medium blue row and a medium blue square in the dark blue row. Refer to the quilt photo, (page 48).

4. Repeat Steps 1 and 2 to make 1 row of medium blue squares, 1 row of mixed medium and light blue squares, and 1 row of light blue squares.

5. You will have a total of 5 rows of 26 squares 3½" × 3½".

12-Patch Blocks

1. With right sides together, stitch a row of 3 dark blue 3½" × 3½" squares together. Press the seam allowances.

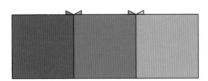

2. Repeat to make 16 units of 3 squares each.

3. Stitch a set of 3-square units from Step 2 to another set of 3-square units along the 9½" edge, matching the seams. Press the seam allowances.

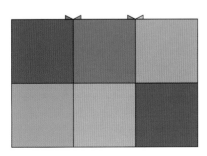

4. Repeat to make 8 units of 6 squares.

5. Stitch a unit of 6 dark blue squares to a second unit of 6 dark blue squares along the 9½" edge. Press the seam allowances.

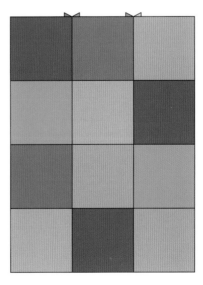

6. Repeat Step 5 to make 4 units of 12 patches.

7. Repeat Steps 1–6 to make 4 units of 12 patches using medium blue squares and 2 units of 12 patches using light blue squares.

4-Patch Half-Square Triangle Blocks

4-Patch Units

1. With right sides together, stitch 2 dark blue 3½" × 3½" squares.

2. Repeat Step 1 and press the seam allowances.

3. Make a 4-patch unit using the pairs of squares from Steps 1 and 2.

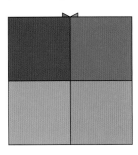

4. Repeat Steps 1–3 to make 9 dark blue 4-patch units.

5. Repeat Steps 1–3 to make 9 medium blue 4-patch units.

6. Repeat Steps 1–3 to make 3 light blue 4-patch units.

Combine the 4-Patch Units with the Half-Square Triangle Units

Note The orientation of the half-square triangles within the combined 4-patch half-square triangle blocks changes. Some of the units have the half-square triangle in the upper left corner and some of them have it in the upper right. Refer to the quilt assembly diagram (page 58).

1. Stitch 3 dark blue 4-patch units and a dark blue half-square triangle unit to make a 4-patch / Half-square Triangle unit. Press the seam allowances.

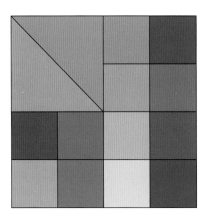

2. Repeat Step 1 to make 2 more dark blue 4-patch / half-square triangle units noting the orientation in the quilt photo (page 48).

3. Stitch a 4-patch / square unit using 4-patch blocks and a 6½" × 6½" medium blue square. Press the seam allowances.

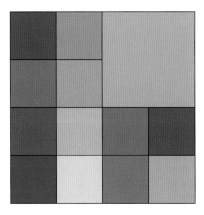

4. Stitch 3 medium blue 4-patch blocks together with a dark blue half-square triangle unit. Press the seam allowances.

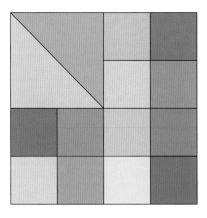

5. Stitch 3 medium blue 4-patch units together with a medium blue half-square triangle block. Press the seam allowances.

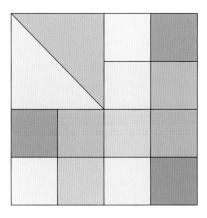

6. Repeat Step 5 to make a total of 2 medium blue 4-patch half-square triangle blocks.

7. Repeat Step 5 using 3 light blue 4 patch units and 1 light blue half-square triangle block.

Stitching the Pieced Top Together

Make the Rows

Following the quilt assembly diagram (page 58) stitch the blocks into rows.

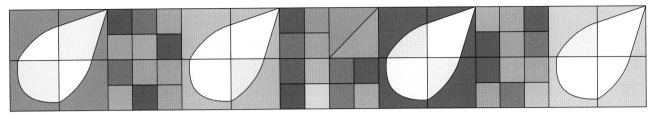

Row 1

Make the Sections for Quilt As-You-Go

Section 1

1. Section 1 includes Row 1, a row of 26 dark blue 3½″ squares, Row 2, and a second row of 26 dark blue 3½″ squares.

2. Stitch these rows together and press the seam allowances.

Section 2

1. Section 2 includes Row 3, a row of 26 medium blue 3½″ squares, Row 4, and a row of 26 medium and light blue 3½″ squares.

2. Stitch these rows together and press the seam allowances.

Section 3

1. Section 3 includes Row 5 and a row of 26 light blue squares.

2. Stitch these rows together and press the seam allowances.

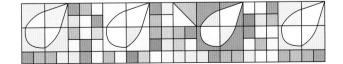

Cloud Row

The Cloud Row will be quilted separately. Be sure that it is centered over the first section and that it is the same length before quilting any of the sections.

If it is slightly shorter, measure how much you need at both ends and cut 2 coping strips that are the width plus a ¼″ seam allowance. The coping strips should measure the same height as the cloud strip.

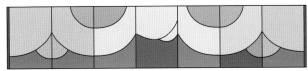

Quilt As-You-Go

1. Layer the Cloud Row quilt top, the Cloud batting rectangle, and the Cloud backing rectangle.

2. Repeat Step 1 for Sections 1, 2, and 3. See Layering Columnar Sections (page 13).

3. Baste each section. See Basting Columnar Sections (page 13).

4. Quilt in your desired pattern.

5. Join the sections according to the instructions in Joining/Seaming Columnar Sections, page 14).

6. Trim away any excess fabric from the edges of the quilt (see Finishing and Trimming, page 23).

7. Bind the quilt using your preferred method.

Quilt assembly

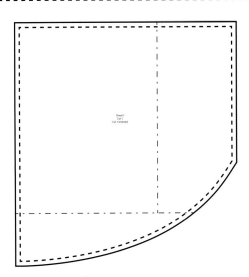

To make the complete pattern, join the pattern pieces following the diagram for reference.

Rainy Days and Scrap Quilts
Cloud 1
Cut 1.
Cut 1 reversed.

Part A

Join B here.

Join C here

Rainy Days and Scrap Quilts
Cloud 1

Part B

Join A here.

Join C here.

Join A/B here.

Rainy Days and Scrap Quilts
Cloud 1

Part C

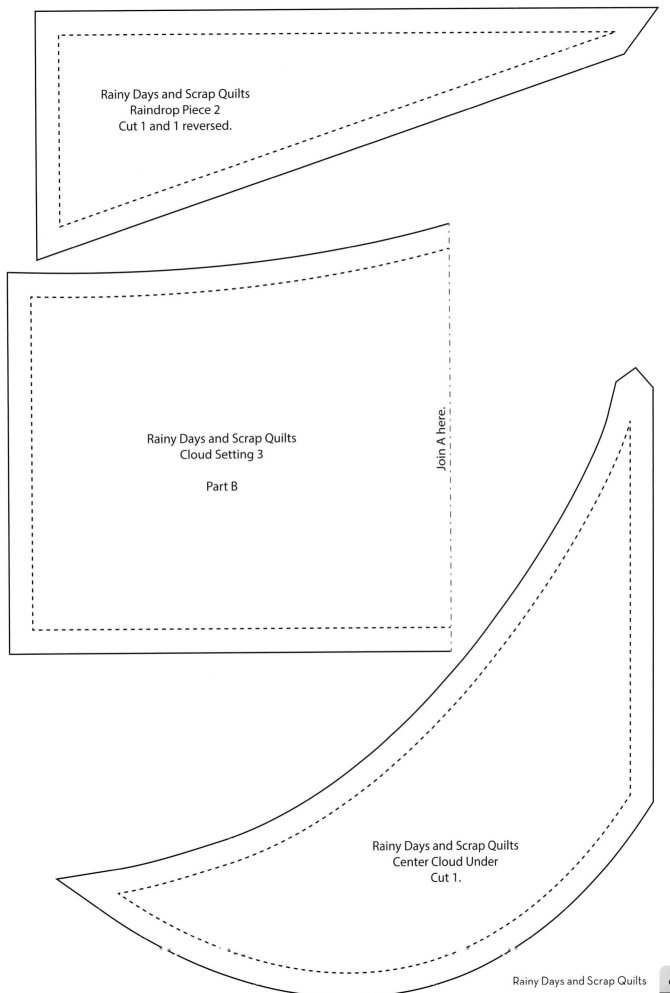

Rainy Days and Scrap Quilts
Raindrop Piece 2
Cut 1 and 1 reversed.

Rainy Days and Scrap Quilts
Cloud Setting 3

Part B

Join A here.

Rainy Days and Scrap Quilts
Center Cloud Under
Cut 1.

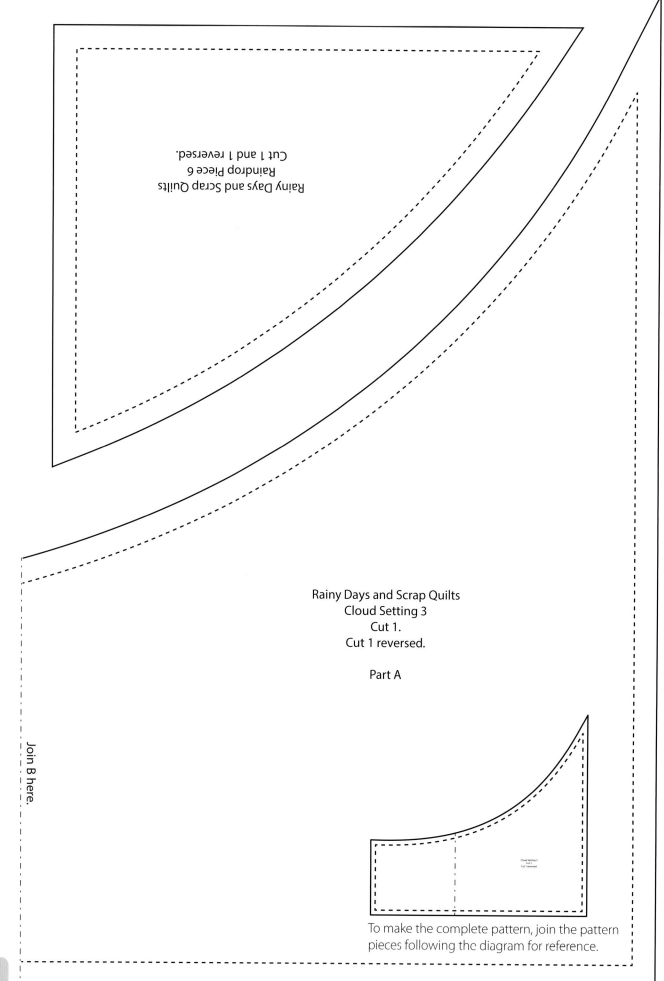

Rainy Days and Scrap Quilts
Raindrop Piece 6
Cut 1 and 1 reversed.

Rainy Days and Scrap Quilts
Cloud Setting 3
Cut 1.
Cut 1 reversed.

Part A

Join B here.

Cloud Setting 3
Cut 1.
Cut 1 reversed.

To make the complete pattern, join the pattern
pieces following the diagram for reference.

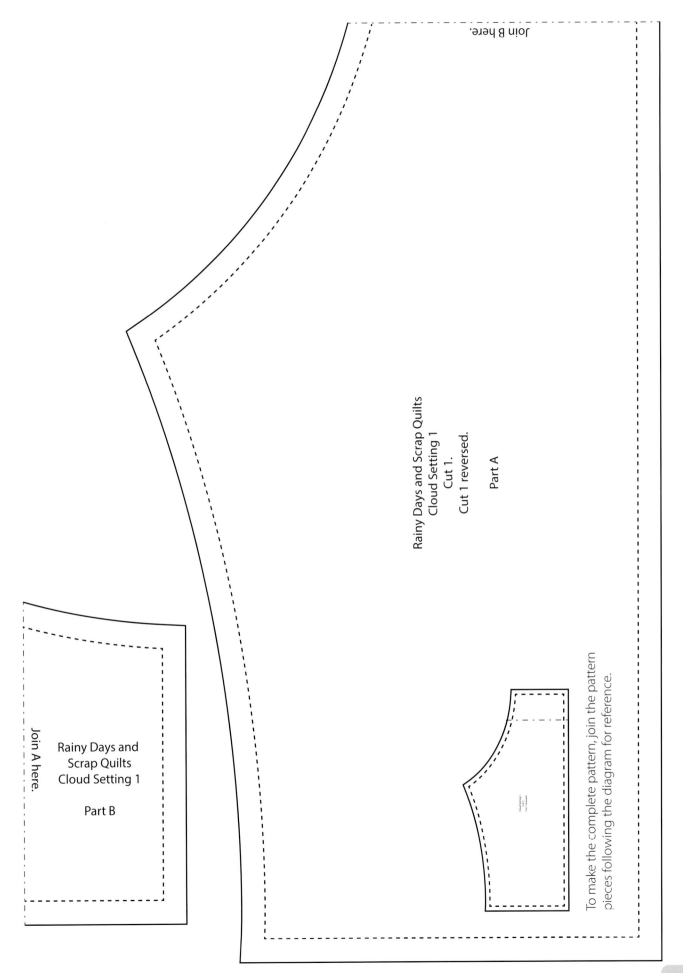

Join B here.

Join B here.

Rainy Days and Scrap Quilts
Cloud Setting 1
Cut 1.
Cut 1 reversed.

Part A

Join A here.

Rainy Days and
Scrap Quilts
Cloud Setting 1

Part B

To make the complete pattern, join the pattern
pieces following the diagram for reference.

Rainy Days and Scrap Quilts
Cloud Setting Center
Cut 1.

Part A

Join B here.

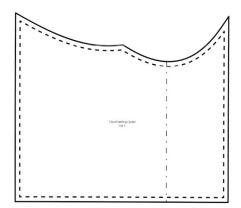

To make the complete pattern, join the pattern
pieces following the diagram for reference.

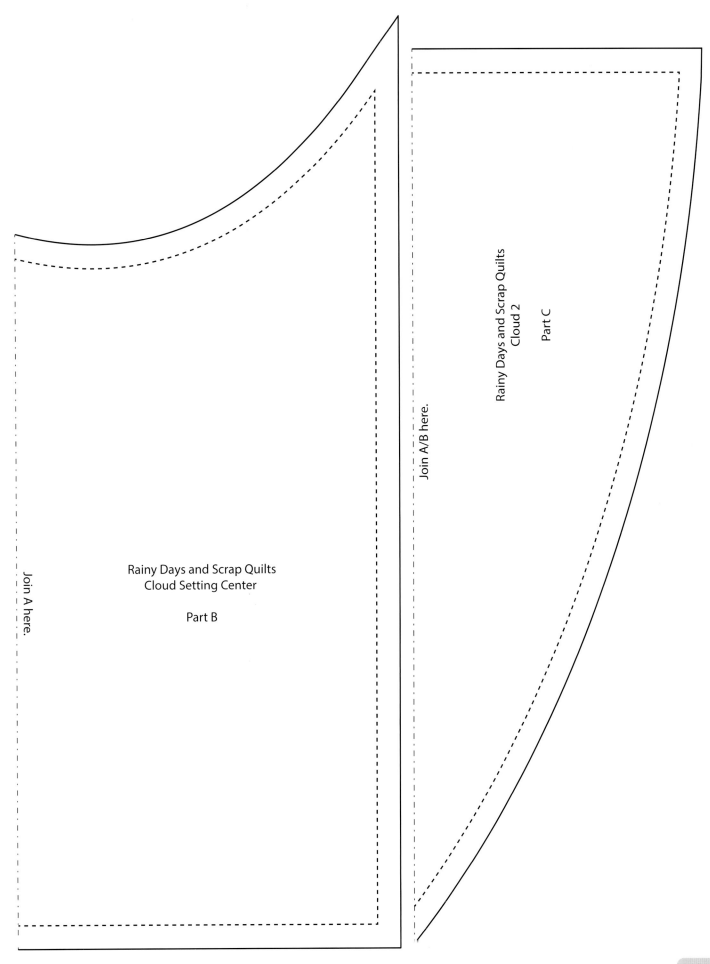

Rainy Days and Scrap Quilts
Cloud 2

Part C

Join A/B here.

Rainy Days and Scrap Quilts
Cloud Setting Center

Part B

Join A here.

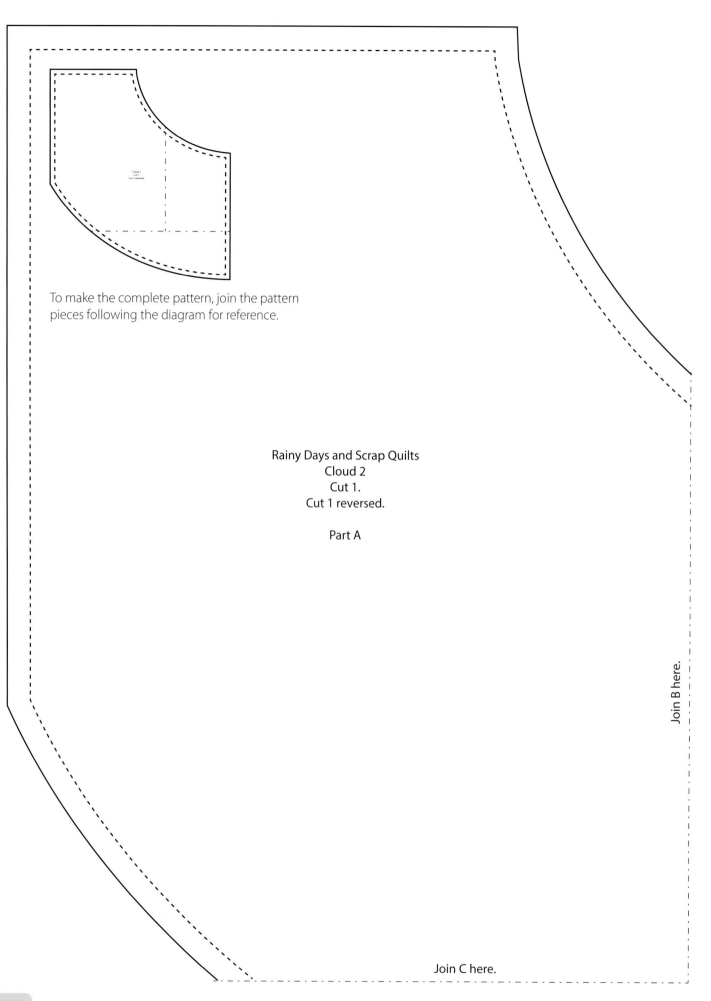

To make the complete pattern, join the pattern
pieces following the diagram for reference.

Rainy Days and Scrap Quilts
Cloud 2
Cut 1.
Cut 1 reversed.

Part A

Join B here.

Join C here.

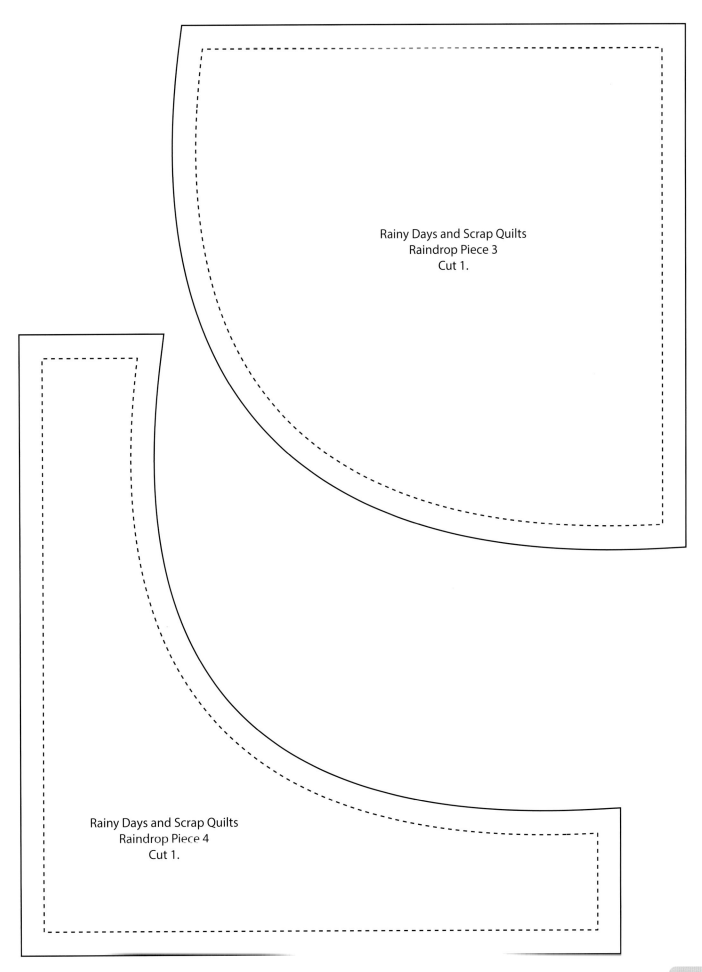

Rainy Days and Scrap Quilts
Raindrop Piece 3
Cut 1.

Rainy Days and Scrap Quilts
Raindrop Piece 4
Cut 1.

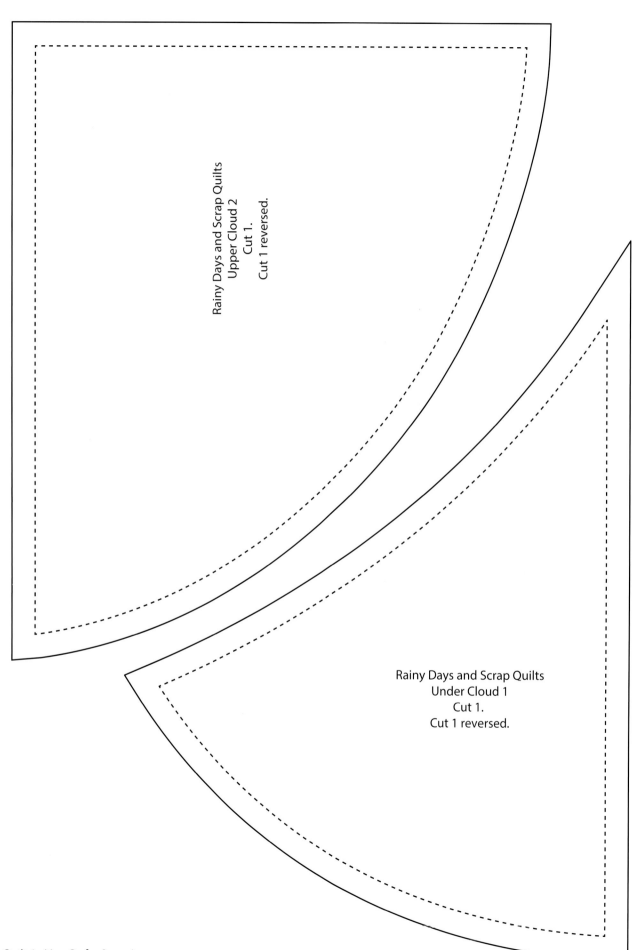

Rainy Days and Scrap Quilts
Upper Cloud 2
Cut 1.
Cut 1 reversed.

Rainy Days and Scrap Quilts
Under Cloud 1
Cut 1.
Cut 1 reversed.

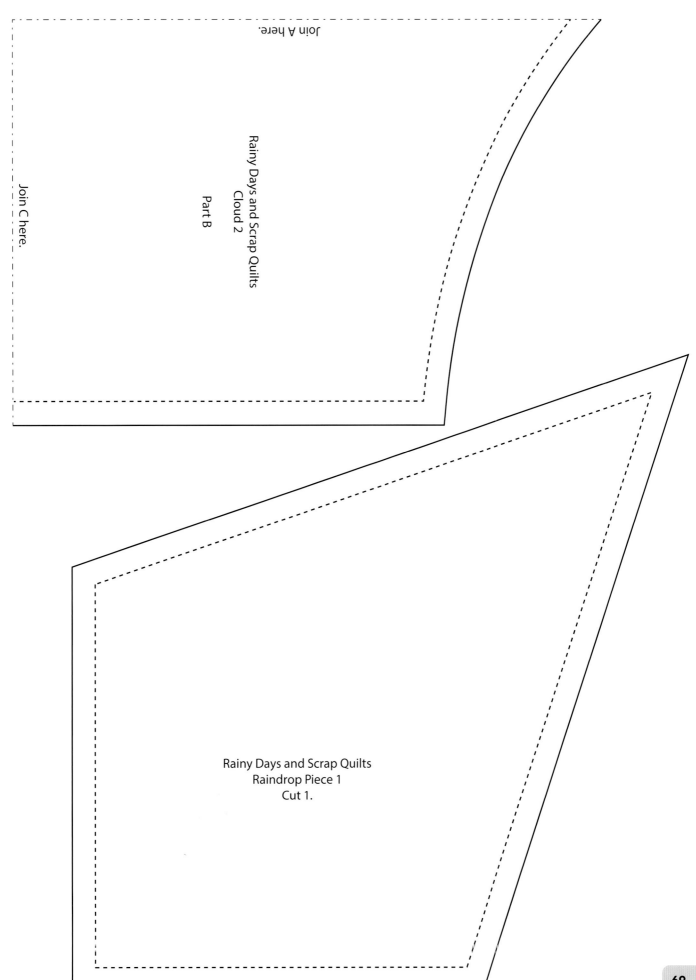

Join A here.

Join C here.

Rainy Days and Scrap Quilts
Cloud 2

Part B

Rainy Days and Scrap Quilts
Raindrop Piece 1
Cut 1.

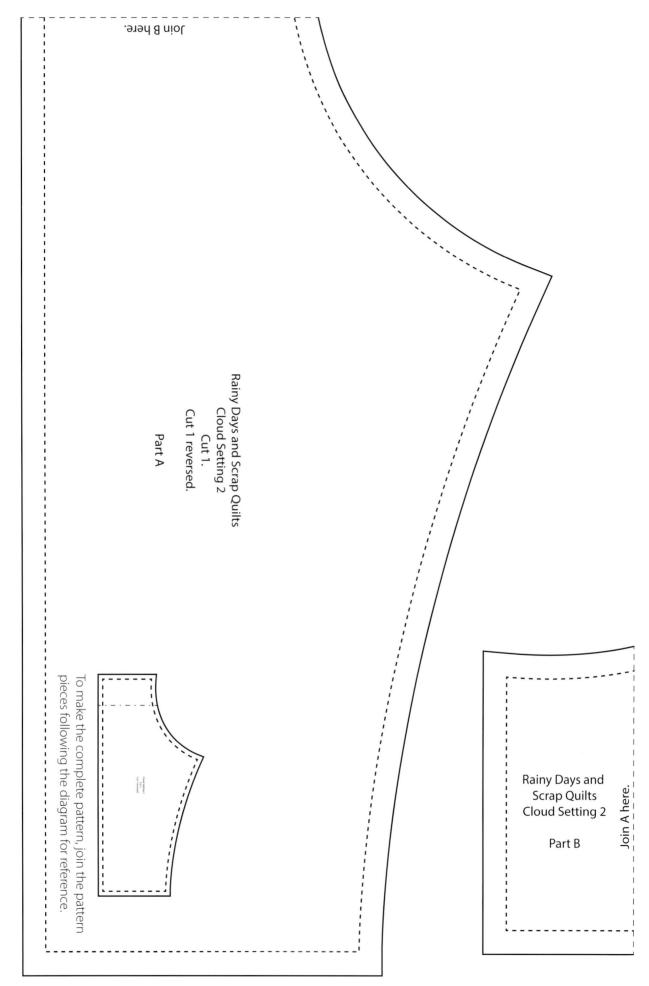

Rainy Days and Scrap Quilts
Cloud Setting 2
Cut 1.
Cut 1 reversed.

Part A

Join B here.

Join B here.

To make the complete pattern, join the pattern pieces following the diagram for reference.

Rainy Days and
Scrap Quilts
Cloud Setting 2

Part B

Join A here.

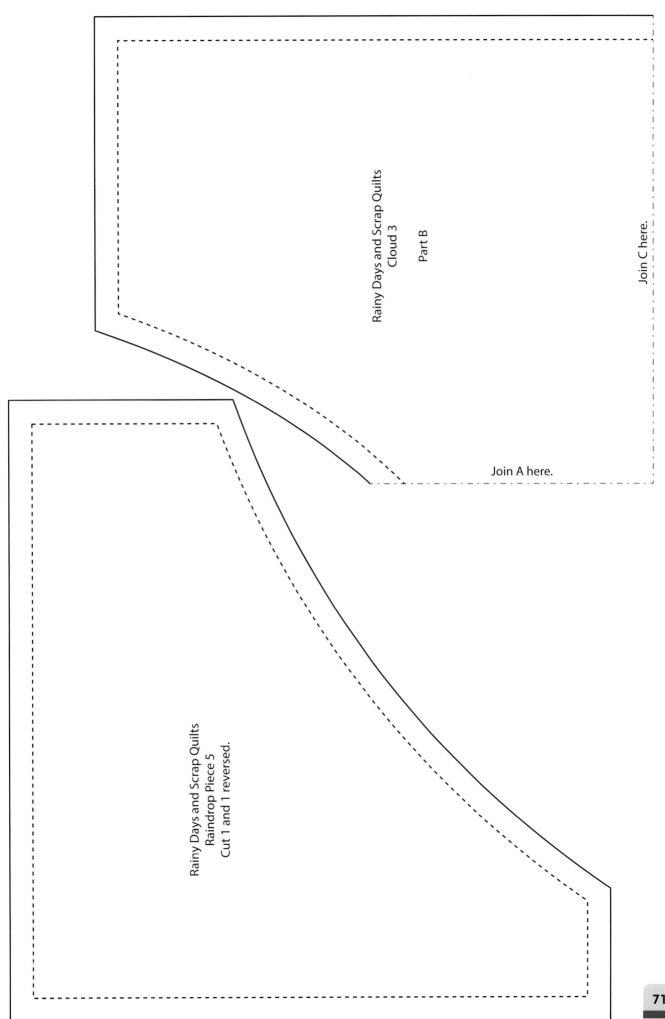

Rainy Days and Scrap Quilts
Cloud 3
Part B

Join C here.

Join A here.

Rainy Days and Scrap Quilts
Raindrop Piece 5
Cut 1 and 1 reversed.

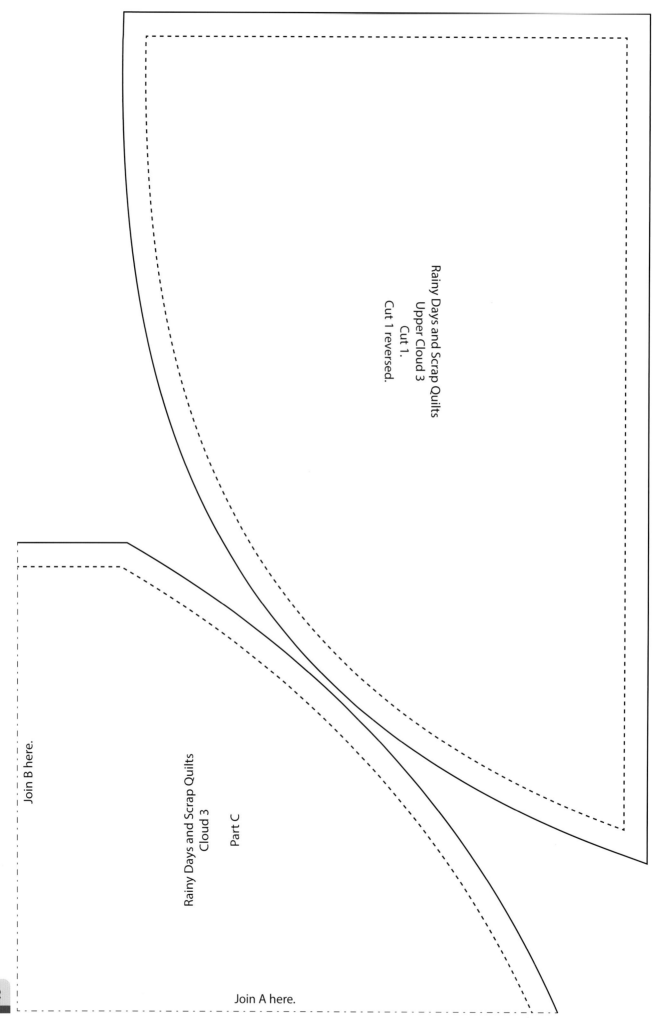

Rainy Days and Scrap Quilts
Upper Cloud 3
Cut 1.
Cut 1 reversed.

Join B here.

Rainy Days and Scrap Quilts
Cloud 3

Part C

Join A here.

Join B/C here.

Rainy Days and Scrap Quilts
Cloud 3
Cut 1.
Cut 1 reversed.

Part A

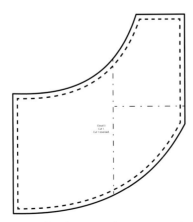

To make the complete pattern, join the pattern
pieces following the diagram for reference.

Rainy Days and Scrap Quilts
Center Cloud

Part B

Join A here.

Rainy Days and Scrap Quilts
Under Cloud 2
Cut 1.
Cut 1 Reversed.

Center Cloud
Cut 1.

To make the complete pattern, join the pattern
pieces following the diagram for reference.

Rainy Days and Scrap Quilts
Center Cloud
Cut 1.

Part A

Join B here.

You've Got a Friend

FINISHED BLOCK: 12″ × 12″ ◆ **FINISHED QUILT:** 96½″ × 96½″

This is a simple Bear's Paw quilt, but it also looks like a Maple Leaf quilt without the appliquéd stems. I like it that way … no appliqué! It's large enough to cover a queen-sized bed with a drop on both sides.

We have all four seasons in Wisconsin, and I like it that way. I could never leave my all-season state!

Materials

The scrap sizes should be at least 4½″ × 4½″ or 5½″ × 5½″.

ASSORTED SCRAPS

Light gray: ½ yard total

Medium gray: ¾ yard total

Dark gray: ¾ yard total

Light blue: ¼ yard total

White: 2 yards total

Off-white: 2 yards total

Pink: ¾ yard total

Light spring green: ⅝ yard total

Dark spring green: ⅝ yard total

Brown: ½ yard total

Orange: ½ yard total

Gold: ⅛ yard total

Beige: ¾ yard total

Green: 1⅛ yards total

Orange-red: ¾ yard total

CENTER SASHING

Tan (front): ¼ yard

Red (backing): ¼ yard

BATTING

6 yards of 60″-wide

BACKING

Winter: 3 yards

Spring: 3 yards

Summer: 3 yards

Fall: 3 yards

BINDING

⅞ yard

Cutting

WINTER

Light, medium, and dark grays
Cut 19 squares 5½" × 5½" dark and medium.
Cut 18 squares 5½" × 5½" light.
Cut 49 squares 4½" × 4½" dark and medium.

Light blue
Cut 3 squares 5½" × 5½".
Cut 2 squares 4½" × 4½".

White and off-white prints
Cut 24 squares 5½" × 5½".
Cut 29 squares 4½" × 4½".

SPRING

Pink
Cut 20 squares 5½" × 5½".
Cut 10 squares 4½" × 4½".

Light and dark spring green
Cut 20 squares 5½" × 5½".
Cut 40 squares 4½" × 4½".

White and off-white prints
Cut 24 squares 5½" × 5½".
Cut 30 squares 4½" × 4½".

SUMMER

Greens
Cut 20 squares 5½" × 5½".
Cut 40 squares 4½" × 4½".

Orange-Reds
Cut 20 squares 5½" × 5½".
Cut 10 squares 4½" × 4½".

White and off-white prints
Cut 24 squares 5½" × 5½".
Cut 30 squares 4½" × 4½".

FALL

Brown, orange, and gold
Cut 20 squares 5½" × 5½".
Cut 40 squares 4½" × 4½".

Beige
Cut 20 squares 5½" × 5½".
Cut 10 squares 4½" × 4½".

White and off-white prints
Cut 24 squares 5½" × 5½".
Cut 30 squares 4½" × 4½".

CENTER SASHING

Tan
Cut 4 strips 1½" × width of fabric.

Red
Cut 4 strips 1¼" × width of fabric.

BATTING

Cut 4 rectangles 52" × 60".

BACKING

Cut the backing for each season into 2 rectangles 54" × width of fabric.

BINDING

Cut 11 strips 2½" × width of fabric.

Block Construction

All seam allowances are ¼″ wide and pressed open unless otherwise noted.

Winter

1. With right sides together, layer a light gray 5½″ × 5½″ square with a dark gray 5½″ × 5½″ square.

2. Draw a diagonal line from one corner to the opposite corner on the top square.

3. Stitch ¼″ on both sides of the line.

4. Cut along the line.

5. Open and press the seam allowances. This will yield 2 half-square triangle units.

6. Square the half-square triangles to 4½″ × 4½″, making certain that the diagonal line on the template rests on the diagonal line of the half-square triangle.

7. Pair a light blue 5½″ × 5½″ square with a dark gray or medium gray and make 2 half square triangles.

8. Repeat to make 40 half-square triangle units using the assortment of dark, medium, and light gray 5½″ × 5½″ squares.

9. Stitch 2 half-square triangles, right sides together, along one edge with the orientation shown below. Make sure to place the darks in the upper right.

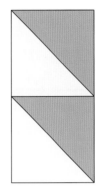

10. Stitch a light gray 4½″ × 4½″ square to the 2 half-square triangle unit.

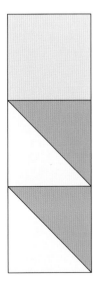

11. Stitch together 2 squares 4½″ × 4½″ of the light, medium, or dark gray.

12. Add a half-square triangle unit to one end of the 4½″ × 4½″ squares. Note the orientation in relation to the row of squares sewn in Step 9.

13. Repeat Steps 11 and 12.

14. Stitch the 3 rows of squares together as shown.

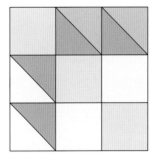

15. Repeat Steps 8–13 to make 10 Winter blocks.

16. Repeat Steps 1–14 using the white and off-white prints to make 6 neutral blocks.

17. Arrange the blocks as shown.

18. Stitch the blocks into rows and stitch the rows together.

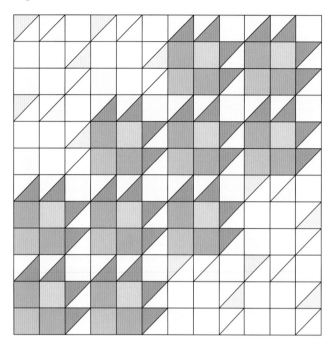

Spring

Refer to quilt photo for placement (page 76) and repeat Steps 1–17 of Winter (pages 79–80) to make the Spring section of the quilt, using the pink and spring green squares.

Summer

Refer to the quilt photo for placement (page 76) and repeat Steps 1–17 of Winter (pages 79–80) to make the Summer section of the quilt, using the green and orange-red squares.

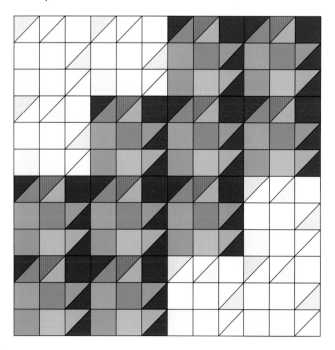

Fall

Refer to the quilt photo (page 76) for placement and repeat Steps 1–17 of Winter (pages 79–80) to make the Fall section of the quilt, using the brown, orange, and gold squares.

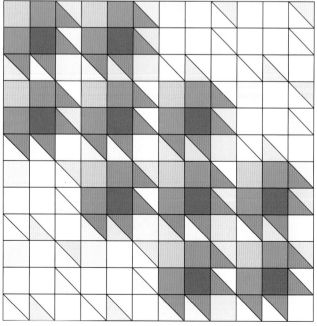

Quilt As-You-Go

1. With right sides together, stitch the 2 backing rectangles together along the selvage edge, using a ⅝″ seam allowance.

2. Press the seam allowances open. The backing piece will now measure 54″ × 88″.

3. Trim the backing piece so that it measures 54″ × 54″.

4. Repeat Steps 1–3 for the other 3 backings.

5. Layer each quarter section with batting and backing and baste (see Layering Columnar Sections, page 13, and Basting Columnar Sections, page 13).

6. Quilt the sections.

7. Follow all directions in Joining Quarter Sections (page 17) to join the sections with the center sashing strips.

8. Trim and bind your quilt using your preferred method (see Finishing and Trimming, page 23).

Quilt assembly

Reverse Churn Dash

FINISHED BLOCK: 10" × 10"   ◆   **FINISHED QUILT:** 80½" × 80½"

What I love about this quilt is that it's just a simple X and O quilt. But, as with many great quilting patterns, multiple designs often appear. You may see an X and O quilt, and you may see an alteration of a churn dash block. When you back up, it can look a little like lightning strikes!

This quilt has an adjacent (analogous) color scheme. The pinks and corals initially may fool you into thinking it has a monochromatic scheme, but pink and coral are simply tints of pink and orange, which are color wheel neighbors!

Materials

Pink, coral, and gold: 5½ yards total of assorted scraps at least the cut sizes below

White: 5½ yards

Batting: 2½ yards of 90″-wide

Backing: 7¼ yards

Binding: ¾ yard

Cutting

Pink, coral, and gold
Cut 128 squares 5½″ × 5½″.
Cut 256 squares 3½″ × 3½″.

White
Cut 19 strips 5½″ × width of fabric.
  Subcut 128 squares 5½″ × 5½″.
Cut 24 strips 3½″ × width of fabric.
  Subcut 256 squares 3½″ × 3½″.

Batting
Cut 2 rectangles 33″ × 83″.
Cut 1 rectangle 23″ × 83″.

Backing
Cut 2 rectangles 37″ × 87″.
Cut 1 rectangle 27″ × 87″.

Binding
Cut 9 strips 2½″ × width of fabric.

Make the Blocks

X Blocks

All seam allowances are ¼″ wide and pressed open unless otherwise noted.

1. With right sides together and matching the edges, lay a 3½″ × 3½″ colored square on the corner of a white square 5½″ × 5½″.

2. Draw a diagonal line from one side corner to the other side corner on the colored square.

3. Repeat Steps 1 and 2 for the opposite colored corner.

4. Stitch on the diagonal lines.

5. Cut ¼″ outside of the stitching.

TIP

If you stitch a hair's width outside of the diagonal line, you will have much greater accuracy when the fabric is folded to the outside. There is a small amount of space taken up by the folding over of the fabric that will prevent it from being a perfect 5½″ × 5½″ square. Stitching just off to the side of the diagonal line will allow space for that fold.

6. Open the colored triangle on both sides and press the seam allowances toward the colored triangle.

7. Repeat Steps 1–6 to make 128 blocks 5½" × 5½".

8. Layer 2 blocks, right sides together, noting the orientation and stitch.

9. Open and press the seam allowances.

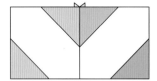

10. Repeat Steps 8 and 9 to make a second block unit.

11. Join the 2 block units created in Steps 8–10, right sides together, matching center seams. Note the orientation.

12. Stitch the blocks together.

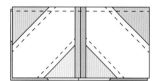

13. Open and press the seam allowances.

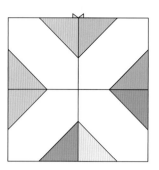

14. Repeat Steps 8–13 to create 32 X blocks.

O Blocks

1. With right sides together and matching the edges, place a 3½" × 3½" white square on the corner of a 5½" × 5½" colored square.

2. Draw a diagonal line from one side corner to the other side corner of the white square.

3. Repeat Steps 1 and 2 for the opposite white corner.

4. Stitch on the diagonal lines.

5. Cut ¼" outside of the stitching.

6. Open the white triangle on both sides and press the seam allowances toward the colored square.

7. Repeat Steps 1–6 to make 128 blocks 5½" × 5½".

8. Layer 2 of the blocks, right sides together, noting the orientation and stitch.

9. Open and press the seam allowances.

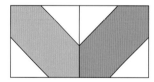

10. Repeat Steps 8 and 9 to make a second block unit.

11. Stitch the 2 block units from Steps 8–10, matching the center seams. Note the orientation.

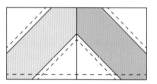

12. Open and press the seam allowances.

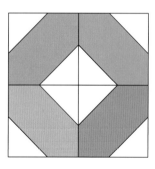

13. Repeat Steps 8–12 to create 32 O blocks.

Make the Rows

1. With right sides together and matching seams, stitch an X block to an O block.

2. Press the seam allowances.

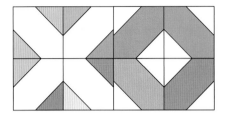

3. Continue to stitch the X and O blocks together until there are 8 in a row.

4. Press the seam allowances.

5. Repeat Steps 1–4 to make 8 rows. Start every row by alternating the X's and Os. Refer to the quilt photo (page 82).

Make the Sections

1. Stitch 2 rows together starting with an X row for the first row, matching the seams.

2. Stitch a third row to the first 2, making certain to alternate the rows for this section 1.

3. Press the seam allowances and set it aside.

4. Repeat Steps 1 and 3 for Section 2.

5. Repeat Steps 1–3 for Section 3.

Quilt As-You-Go

1. Layer Sections 1 and 3 with the wider cuts of batting and backing and baste (see Layering Columnar Sections, page 13, and Basting Columnar Sections, page 13).

2. Layer Section 2 with the narrower cuts of batting and backing and baste (see Layering Columnar Sections, page 13, and Basting Columnar Sections, page 13).

3. Quilt in columnar fashion (see Quilting Columnar Sections, page 14).

4. Join the sections (see Joining/Seaming Columnar Sections, page 14).

5. Trim away any excess fabric from the edges of the quilt (see Finishing and Trimming, page 23).

6. Bind the quilt using your preferred method.

Quilt assembly

Payson

FINISHED BLOCK: 5″ × 5″ ◆ **FINISHED QUILT:** 50½″ × 50½″

I had been thinking of this quilt for about a year before I made it. I had taken a shortcut driving home from Tucson, cutting across the corner of Arizona, and found myself driving through the Tonto National Forest. The drive was scary and treacherous as it took me through the mountains, with some horrible hairpin turns and steep drops. When I finally got through it, I found myself in a town named Payson. It was such a relief to see those pine trees and find that I was out of the mountains.

The secret to success for this quilt is creating an ombré effect with your scraps. I used a green that leaned more blue than yellow. When I see forests of pine trees, they always look blue to me.

Materials

Light green: 1½ yards total of assorted scraps at least the cut sizes below

Medium green: 1½ yards total of assorted scraps at least the cut sizes below

Dark green: 2⅛ yards total of assorted scraps at least the cut sizes below

Batting: 1⅝ yards of 60″-wide

Backing: 3½ yards

Binding: ½ yard

Cutting

Light green
Cut 30 squares 5½″ × 5½″.
Cut 60 squares 3½″ × 3½″.

Medium green
Cut 30 squares 5½″ × 5½″.
Cut 60 squares 3½″ × 3½″.

Dark green
Cut 40 squares 5½″ × 5½″.
Cut 80 squares 3½″ × 3½″.

Batting
Cut 1 rectangle 33″ × 53″.
Cut 1 rectangle 23″ × 53″.

Backing
Cut 1 rectangle 37″ × 57″.
Cut 1 rectangle 27″ × 57″.

Binding
Cut 6 strips 2½″ × width of fabric.

Make the Blocks

All seam allowances are 1/4" wide and pressed open unless otherwise noted.

1. Place a 3½" × 3½" dark green square on the upper left corner of a dark green 5½" × 5½" square, matching the edges.

2. Draw a diagonal line from one edge corner to the opposite edge corner.

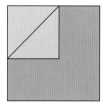

3. Stitch on the line.

TIP

If you stitch a hair's width outside of the diagonal line, you will have much greater accuracy when the fabric is folded to the outside. There is a small amount of space taken up by the folding over of the fabric that will prevent it from being a perfect 5½" × 5½" square. Stitching just off to the side of the diagonal line will allow space for that fold.

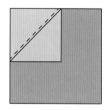

4. Trim ¼" from the stitched line on the outside of the square.

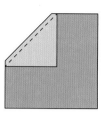

5. Repeat Steps 1–4 for the lower right corner of the 5½" × 5½" square.

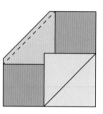

6. Open and press the seam allowances.

7. Repeat Steps 1–6 using all the dark green squares moving into the medium green squares, and finally the light green squares.

Make the Columns

Note Each column has 10 pairs of blocks: 4 dark pairs, 3 medium pairs, and 3 light pairs. It's possible that your quilt may have more lights than darks, depending on your fabric selection. The important part is that each column moves from dark to light. Columns 2 and 4 are rotated after completion.

1. Layer 2 completed dark blocks, right sides together, matching the edges.

2. Stitch along one edge.

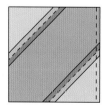

3. Open and press the seam allowances.

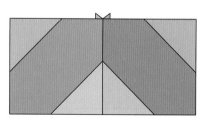

4. Repeat Steps 1–3 to make a total of 4 pairs of dark blocks. Refer to the quilt photo (page 86).

5. Repeat Steps 1–3 to make 3 pairs of medium blocks.

6. Repeat Steps 1–3 to make 3 pairs of light blocks.

7. Stitch the blocks along the long 10½″ edges to create a column of 10 pairs of blocks.

8. Repeat Step 7 to make 5 columns.

Lay Out the Columns

1. Refer to the quilt assembly diagram and place 3 of the columns with the dark blocks at the top, and 2 of the columns with the light blocks at the top.

2. Stitch 3 columns together, matching the seams and keeping the columns in order.

3. Press the seam allowances.

4. Stitch the remaining 2 columns together, matching the seams and keeping them in order.

5. Press the seam allowances.

Quilt As-You-Go

1. Layer the 3-column section together with the wider piece of backing fabric and the wider piece of batting (see Layering Columnar Sections, page 13).

2. Baste in your preferred manner (see Basting Columnar Sections, page 13).

3. Layer the 2-column section together with the smaller piece of backing fabric and the smaller piece of batting and baste.

4. Quilt in columnar fashion (see Quilting Columnar Sections, page 14).

5. Trim away any excess fabric from the edges of the quilt.

6. Join the sections (see Joining/Seaming Columnar Sections, page 14)

7. Trim away any excess fabric from the edges of the quilt (see Finishing and Trimming, page 23).

8. Bind the quilt using your preferred method.

Quilt assembly

Frank is Always Wright

FINISHED BLOCK: 4″ × 4″ ◆ **FINISHED QUILT:** 70½″ × 72½″

My intention with this quilt was to make it look like a Frank Lloyd Wright design. I absolutely love his architectural style. I love the Arts and Crafts architectural movement and the houses, bungalows, and interior design that came from that era.

When I was thinking of a name for this quilt, I also thought of my father, who was also named Frank. He was the strongest, most intelligent man I have ever met. He had so much life experience that when he gave advice, 99 percent of the time, he was right. Even though I didn't appreciate it when I was young, I sure do remember his wise words today. Here's to you, Frank Lloyd Wright, and to you, Daddy.

Materials

Green: 4¼ yards total of assorted scraps at least the cut sizes below

Brown: 1⅝ yards total of assorted scraps at least the cut sizes below

Off-white and white: 5⅞ yards total of assorted scraps at least the cut sizes below

Off-white sashing: 2¼ yards

Olive green solid: ¼ yard

Brown solid: ⅛ yard

Sash-In-A-Dash: 4¼ yards

Batting: 2¼ yards of 90″-wide

Backing: 6¾ yards

Binding: ⅝ yard

Cutting

Green scraps
Cut 72 squares 5½″ × 5½″.
Cut 144 squares 3½″ × 3½″.

Brown scraps
Cut 36 squares 5½″ × 5½″.
Cut 72 squares 3½″ × 3½″.

Off-white and white scraps
Cut 108 squares 5½″ × 5½″.
Cut 216 squares 3½″ × 3½″.

Off-white sashing
Cut 6 strips 3½″ × 72½″ from the length of the fabric.

Sash-In-A-Dash
Cut 2 lengths 72½″ long.

Olive green sashing
Cut 4 strips 1½″ × width of fabric.

Brown solid
Cut 2 strips 1½″ × width of fabric.

Batting
Cut 3 rectangles 26″ × 75″.

Backing
Cut 3 rectangles 30″ × 79″.

Binding
Cut 8 strips 2½″ × width of fabric.

Make the Blocks

All seam allowances are ¼" wide and pressed open unless otherwise noted.

Half-Square Triangles

1. With right sides together, layer an off-white 5½" × 5½" square with a green 5½" × 5½" square.

2. Draw a diagonal line from one corner to the opposite corner.

3. Stitch ¼" on both sides of the line.

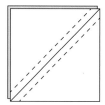

4. Cut on the line.

5. Open and press the seam allowances.

6. Repeat Steps 1–5 to make 144 green/off-white or white half-square triangle units.

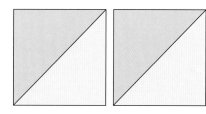

7. Repeat Steps 1–5 to make 72 brown/off-white or white half-square triangle units.

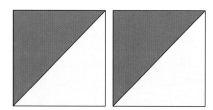

Create the Stripes

1. With right sides together, lay a 3½" × 3½" green square in the corner of the off-white or white half of the green half-square triangle unit, matching edges.

2. Draw a diagonal line from one edge corner to the next.

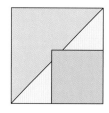

3. Stitch on the diagonal line.

4. Trim the corner ¼" from the stitching.

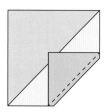

TIP

If you stitch a hair's width outside of the diagonal line, you will have much greater accuracy when the fabric is folded to the outside. There is a small amount of space taken up by the folding over of the fabric that will prevent it from being a perfect 5½" × 5½" square. Stitching just off to the side of the diagonal line will allow space for that fold.

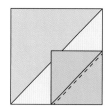

5. Open the corner square and press the seam allowances.

6. Repeat Steps 1–5 using an off-white or white 3½" × 3½" square on top of the green side of the half-square triangle unit.

7. Repeat Steps 1–6 for all 144 of the green and off-white or white half-square triangle units.

8. Square the half-square triangle units to 4½" × 4½", making certain that the diagonal line of the acrylic template or ruler lines up with the diagonal line of the block.

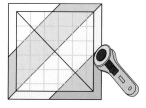

TIP

I recommend using the correct size template. If you are squaring a 4½" × 4½" block, using a 4½" template is easier.

9. Repeat Steps 1–6 using the 72 brown half-square triangle units and the 3½" × 3½" brown squares and the 3½" × 3½" off-white or white squares.

Pair the Units

1. Lay 2 green striped 4½″ × 4½″ units right sides together matching the green corners and stitch together.

2. Open and press the seam allowances.

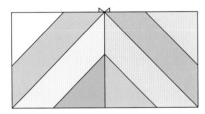

3. Repeat Steps 1 and 2 to make 72 pairs.

4. Repeat Steps 1 and 2 using the brown units, and pair them matching the brown corners. Make 36 pairs.

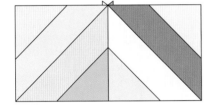

Stitch the Pairs into Columns

Note Note the orientation of the blocks in the quilt photo (page 90) and the quilt assembly diagram (page 95) when putting the pairs together and constructing the columns.

1. Stitch 2 pairs of blocks together, matching the seams. Match the green corners to the edge with the stripes.

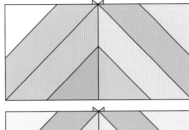

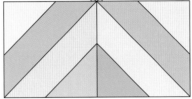
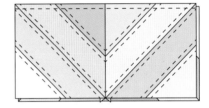

2. Open and press the seam allowances. Orient the blocks as shown.

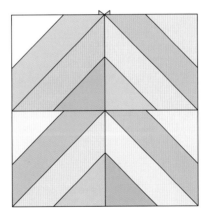

3. Repeat Steps 1 and 2 to make 9 sets of pairs.

4. Refer to the quilt assembly diagram (page 95) and stitch the 9 sets of pairs to make a column. Check to make sure that the column measures 8½″ × 72½″. Adjust seams if needed.

5. Repeat Steps 1–4 for a total of 4 green columns.

6. Repeat Steps 1–4 to make 2 brown columns.

Prepare the Sashing

1. Place 2 olive green 1½" × width of fabric strips, right sides together, perpendicular to one another.

2. Draw a diagonal line from the upper left corner to the lower right corner.

3. Stitch on the line.

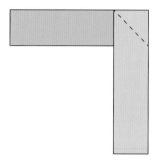

4. Trim ¼" beyond the seam allowance.

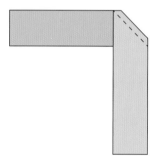

5. Open and press the seam allowance.

6. Trim the sashing to 1½" × 72½".

7. Repeat for a total of 2 olive green sashings and 1 brown sashing.

Sash the Columns

1. Lay the olive green sashing right sides together onto the right edge of 1 green column.

2. Stitch, open, and press the seam allowances toward the sashing.

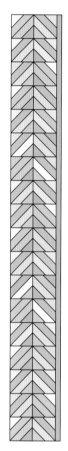

3. Stitch a second green column to the opposite edge of the sashing, making certain that the block orientation is the same as the first column. Refer to the quilt assembly diagram (page 95).

4. Open and press the seam allowances toward the sashing. The column should measure 17½" × 72½".

5. Repeat to make 2 sashed green columns and 1 sashed brown column.

Sew the Large Sashings

1. Refer to the quilt assembly diagram (below right) and stitch a 3½″ × 72½″ strip of off-white sashing to both 72½″ edges of the green columns.

2. Repeat Step 1 for both of the 72½″ edges of the brown column.

TIP

It's important to accurately cut all sashings to the length of your columns. If your columns are made using 4½″ × 4½″ squares, your measurement should be 72½″ after sewing 18 of these together. The sashing and the block columns must match this measurement for the Sash-In-A-dash to fit correctly.

Quilt As-You-Go

1. Layer the quilt top columns with the batting and backing and baste. (See Layering Columnar Sections, page 13, and Basting Columnar Sections, page 13).

2. Quilt in columnar fashion (see Quilting Columnar Sections, page 14). Be sure to quilt to the edges of the sashing or put some additional straight-line quilting in the sashing.

3. Trim away any excess fabric from the edges of the quilt.

4. Join the sections with Sash-In-A-Dash strips (see Sash-In-A-Dash, page 20).

5. Trim away any excess fabric from the edges of the quilt (see Finishing and Trimming, page 23).

6. Bind the quilt using your preferred method.

Quilt assembly

Mountains Majesty

FINISHED BLOCK: 9½" × 9½" ◆ **FINISHED QUILT:** 67¾" × 67¾"

Mountains are the theme of many quilts and they're always pleasing. This quilt uses the Treasure Box Block technique, so it makes quick work of your scraps. It's also set on point, so you can use your new on-point skills for quilt as-you-go.

Materials

White: 2¾ yards

Light gray: ½ yard total of assorted scraps at least 5½" × 5½"

Dark gray: ½ yard total of assorted scraps at least 5½" × 5½"

Turquoise: 2¼ yards total of assorted scraps at least 5½" × 5½"

Batting: 3 yards of 110"-wide

Backing: 7 yards

Binding: ⅝ yard

Cutting

White
Cut 4 strips 9½" × width of fabric.
   Subcut 16 squares 9½" × 9½".
Cut 2 squares 7⅝" × 7⅝".
   Subcut each square on the diagonal to yield 4 corner triangles.
Cut 8 strips 5½" × width of fabric.
   Subcut 50 squares 5½" × 5½".

Light gray
Cut 16 squares 5½" × 5½".

Dark gray
Cut 16 squares 5½" × 5½".

Turquoise
Cut 82 squares 5½" × 5½".

Batting
Cut 1 rectangle 31" × 99".
Cut 2 rectangles 36" × 69".

Backing
Cut 1 rectangle 35" × 103".
Cut 2 rectangles 40" × 73".

Binding
Cut 8 strips 2½" × width of fabric.

Make the Blocks

All seam allowances are ¼" wide and pressed open unless otherwise noted.

1. Using the turquoise and white squares, cut the pieces for the blocks following the directions for The Treasure Box Block, Steps 3–6 (page 26).

2. Follow The Treasure Box Block, Stitching the Block, Steps 1–3 (page 29) to make 50 turquoise and white Treasure Box units and 50 white and turquoise Treasure Box units.

3. Trim the "tail" from the 2" × 5½" rectangle to match the edge of the square. The block should measure 5" × 5".

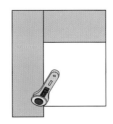

4. Make 25 turquoise and white blocks, noting the orientation.

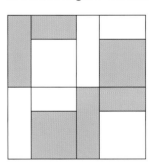

5. Make 8 turquoise / light gray blocks, noting the orientation.

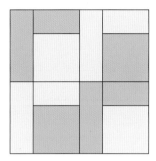

6. Make 8 turquoise / dark gray blocks, noting the orientation.

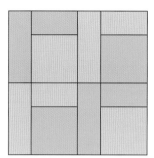

Make the Diagonal Sections

Note Remember that the on-point method of quilt as-you-go is very similar to columnar sectioning, except that the sections are diagonal rows.

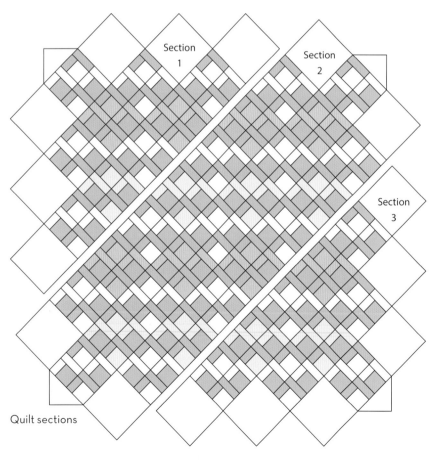

Quilt sections

Section 1

1. With right sides together, stitch a solid white 9½″ × 9½″ square to a turquoise/white block, noting the orientation of the block.

2. With right sides together, stitch a second solid white 9½″ × 9½″ square to the opposite side of the turquoise/white block.

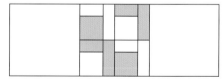

3. Press all seam allowances.

4. Repeat Step 1.

5. Stitch a dark gray / turquoise block to the unit from Step 4.

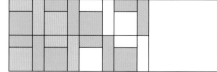

6. Stitch a turquoise/white block to the unit from Step 5.

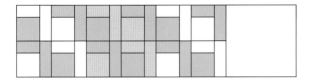

7. Stitch a solid white 9½" × 9½" square to the end of the unit from Step 6.

8. Press all seam allowances.

9. Refer to the quilt sections diagram (page 98) and stitch the third row with 5 blocks and 2 white squares.

10. Refer to the quilt sections diagram (page 98) and sew the rows together, matching the seams.

11. Press all seam allowances. Section 1 is complete, set it aside.

Section 2

1. Refer to the quilt sections diagram (page 98) and stitch together 2 rows with 7 blocks and 2 white squares.

2. Stitch the center row of the section with 9 blocks and a solid white corner triangle at each end.

3. Repeat Section 1, Steps 10 and 11 to assemble Section 2.

Section 3

1. Repeat Section 1, Steps 1–9 (page 98–99).

2. Repeat Section 1, Steps 10 and 11 to assemble Section 3.

3. Stitch a white solid corner triangle to the corner block of Sections 1 and 3, referring to the quilt assembly diagram (below).

Quilt As-You-Go

Refer to On-Point Quilts (page 22).

1. Layer with batting and backing and baste (see Layering Columnar Sections, page 13, and Basting Columnar Sections, page 13).

2. Quilt in columnar fashion (see Quilting Columnar Sections, page 14).

3. Trim away any excess fabric from the edges of the quilt.

4. Join the sections (see Joining/Seaming Columnar Sections, page 14).

5. Trim away any excess fabric from the edges of the quilt (see Finishing and Trimming, page 23).

6. Bind the quilt using your preferred method.

Quilt assembly

Parlor Games

FINISHED BLOCK: 9½" × 7" ◆ **FINISHED QUILT:** 76½" × 77½"

This is pure scrappy fun. This quilt has no color scheme—just line up the same color along the row and it will turn out great. There is enough background space between the colors that if you choose to do so, you can combine multiple colors within the rows.

Sewing curves will be firmly cemented into your repertoire once you finish this quilt. It's easier than you think. Just follow the Sewing Curves instructions from the Rainy Days and Scrap Quilts, Sewing Curves, (page 51) and you'll be good to go.

Materials

The colorful scrap sizes should be at least 6″ × 10″.

Off-white and white background: 5⅞ yards assorted scraps at least 8″ × 11″

Mint: ⅜ yard total of assorted scraps

Orange: ⅜ yard total of assorted scraps

Blue: ⅜ yard total of assorted scraps

Turquoise: ⅜ yard total of assorted scraps

Red: ⅜ yard total of assorted scraps

Yellow-gold: ⅜ yard total of assorted scraps

Navy: ⅜ yard total of assorted scraps

Coral: ⅜ yard total of assorted scraps

Purple: ⅜ yard total of assorted scraps

Pink: ⅜ yard total of assorted scraps

Green: ⅜ yard total of assorted scraps

Batting: 2½ yards of 90″-wide

Backing: 7 yards

Binding: ¾ yard

Cutting

Off-white and white background
Cut 88 using Scallop Background pattern (page 104).

Mint
Cut 8 using Scallop pattern (page 105).

Orange
Cut 8 using Scallop pattern.

Blue
Cut 8 using Scallop pattern.

Turquoise
Cut 8 using Scallop pattern.

Red
Cut 8 using Scallop pattern.

Yellow-gold
Cut 8 using Scallop pattern.

Navy
Cut 8 using Scallop pattern.

Coral
Cut 8 using Scallop pattern.

Purple
Cut 8 using Scallop pattern.

Pink
Cut 8 using Scallop pattern.

Green
Cut 8 using Scallop pattern.

Batting
Cut 2 rectangles 31″ × 79″.
Cut 1 rectangle 24″ × 79″.

Backing
Cut 2 rectangles 35″ × 83″.
Cut 1 rectangle 28″ × 83″.

Binding
Cut 9 strips 2½″ × width of fabric.

Make the Scallop Units

All seam allowances are ¼″ wide and pressed open unless otherwise noted.

1. Follow the instructions for *Rainy Days and Scrap Quilts*, Sewing Curves (page 51).

2. With right sides together, stitch a turquoise scallop to an off-white or white background piece.

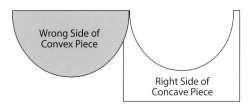

Wrong Side of Convex Piece

Right Side of Concave Piece

3. Press the seam allowances toward the turquoise scallop.

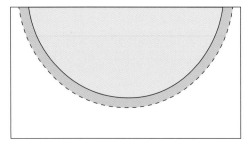

4. Repeat Steps 2 and 3 to make 8 turquoise scallop blocks.

5. Repeat Steps 2–4 for all colors of scallop blocks.

Make the Rows

1. Stitch the 8 turquoise scallop blocks into a row.

2. Press the seam allowances.

3. Repeat Steps 1 and 2 for each color set of scallop blocks.

Make the Sections

1. Refer to the quilt assembly diagram (page 103) to determine the row placement.

2. Stitch the first 4 rows together and press the seam allowances.

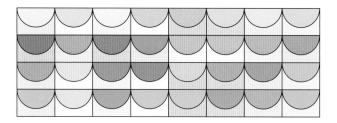

3. Stitch the next 3 rows together and press the seam allowances.

4. Repeat Step 2 to stitch the last 4 rows.

Quilt As-You-Go

1. Layer the first 4-row section with one of the larger batting and backing pieces and baste (see Layering Columnar Sections, page 13, and Basting Columnar Sections, page 13).

2. Repeat Step 1 for the second 4-row section.

3. Layer the 3-row section with the remaining batting and backing and baste.

4. Quilt in columnar fashion (see Quilting Columnar Sections, page 14).

5. Trim away any excess fabric from the edges of the quilt.

6. Join the sections (see Joining/Seaming Columnar Sections, page 14).

7. Trim away any excess fabric from the edges of the quilt (see Finishing and Trimming, page 23).

8. Bind the quilt using your preferred method.

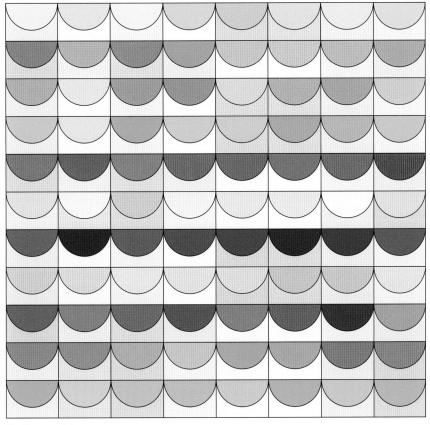

Quilt assembly

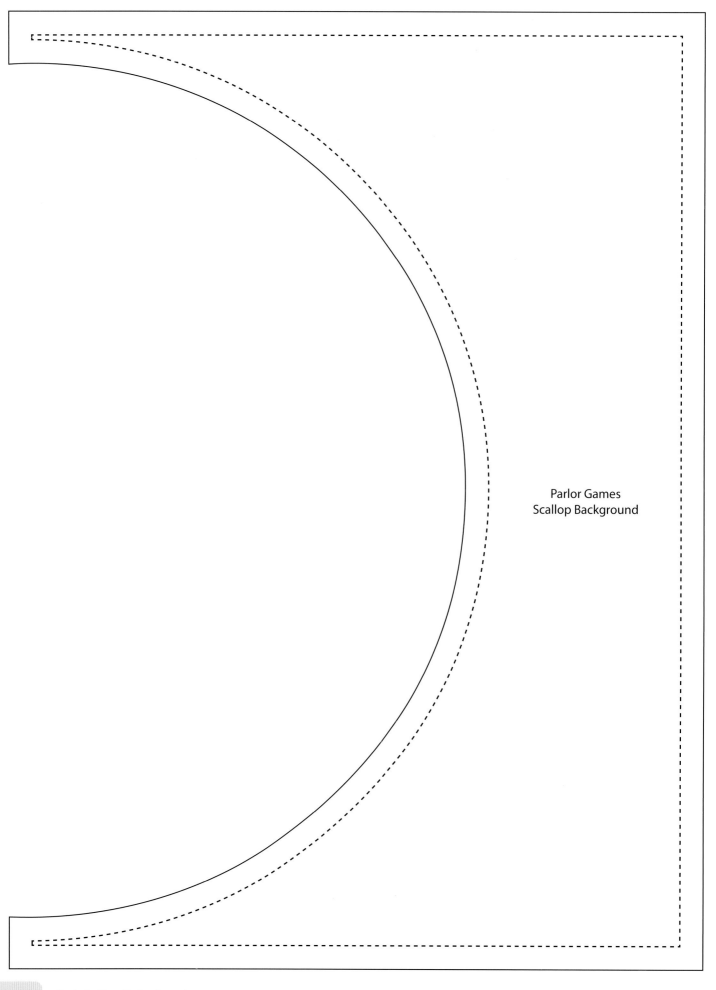

Parlor Games
Scallop Background

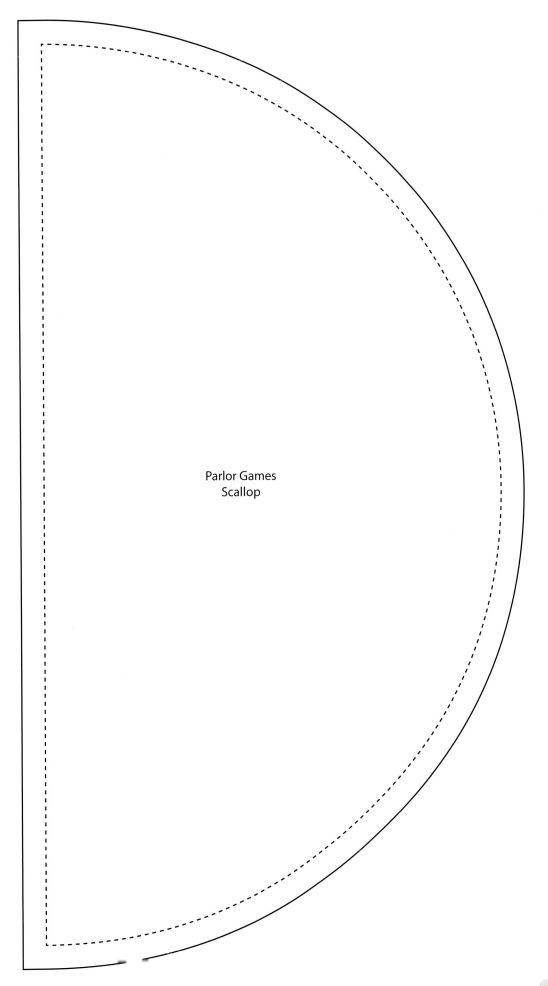

Parlor Games
Scallop

Tucson Sunset

FINISHED BLOCK: 4½" × 4½" ◆ **FINISHED QUILT:** 60" × 60"

These are the colors of the desert mountains in the southwest on a warm, clear night. Amazingly, the mountains can appear purple and coral as the landscape turns to gold.

This quilt has a complementary color scheme. The Tucson Sunset quilt assembly diagram (page 109) uses light purple and dark purple, but the technical colors according to the color wheel are red-violet and purple. It uses the Treasure Box Block (page 26), an incredibly versatile block, and is made using the quarter section quilt as-you-go method (see Quarter Sections, page 17).

Materials

Purple: 1¼ yards total of assorted scraps at least 5½" × 5½"

Coral: 1 yard total of assorted scraps at least 5½" × 5½"

White: ⅝ yard total of assorted scraps at least 5½" × 5½"

Background solid: 2⅛ yards

Center sashing print: ¼ yard

Batting: 2 yards × 72" wide

Backing: 4¼ yards

Binding: ⅝ yard

Cutting

Purple
Cut 48 squares 5½" × 5½".

Coral
Cut 32 squares 5½" × 5½".

White
Cut 16 squares 5½" × 5½".

Background solid
Cut 2 strips 7¼" × width of fabric.
　Subcut 8 squares 7¼" × 7¼".
　Subcut each square on the diagonal to yield 16 corner triangles.
Cut 4 strips 5" × width of fabric.
　Subcut 32 squares 5" × 5".
Cut 16 strips 2½" × width of fabric.

Center sashing print
Cut 4 strips 1½" × width of fabric.

Batting
Cut 4 squares 32" × 32".

Backing
Cut 4 squares 36" × 36".
Cut 4 strips 1¼" × width of fabric for back center sashing.

Binding
Cut 7 strips 2½" × width of fabric.

Make the Sections

All seam allowances are ¼" wide and pressed open unless otherwise noted.

Make the Small Individual Blocks

1. Pair 2 purple squares with 2 coral squares.

2. Refer to The Treasure Box Block, Cutting the Block (page 28) to cut the pieces.

3. Repeat Steps 1 and 2 to cut 3 more sets.

4. Pair 2 white squares with 2 purple squares and repeat Step 2.

5. Repeat Step 2 with a second pair of white and purple squares.

6. Refer to The Treasure Box Block, Stitching the Block, Steps 1–3 (page 29) to sew 8 purple/coral blocks with coral rectangles and 8 purple/coral blocks with purple rectangles.

7. Trim the blocks to 5" × 5".

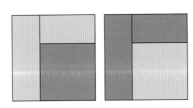

8. Repeat Steps 6 and 7 to sew 4 purple/white blocks with white rectangles and 4 purple/white blocks with purple rectangles.

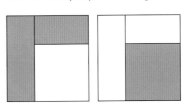

9. Repeat Steps 1–8 to make 3 more sets of blocks.

Make the Large Blocks

1. Stitch 2 purple/coral units with coral rectangles, right sides together.

2. Press the seam allowances.

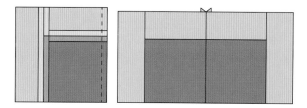

3. Stitch a 5″ × 5″ background square to each end of the pair.

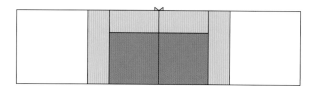

4. Stitch 2 purple/coral units with purple rectangles right sides together.

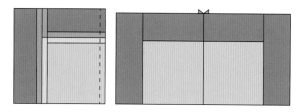

5. Stitch a purple/white unit with white rectangles to each end of the pair from Step 4.

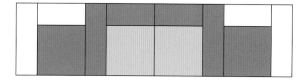

6. Stitch a background 5″ × 5″ square to each end.

7. Stitch the third row of blocks together.

8. Stitch the rows together.

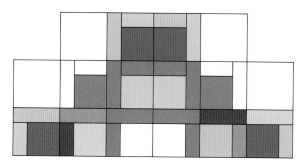

9. Repeat Steps 1–8 to make the second unit.

10. Turn the units so they are mirror images of each other.

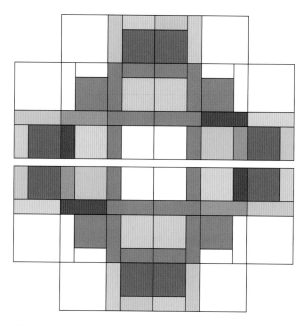

11. Place them right sides together and stitch along the long edge, matching seams.

12. Open and press the seam allowances.

13. Stitch the background triangles to the ends of the blocks.

14. Using a quilting ruler and rotary cutter, trim the background blocks even with the corner triangles.

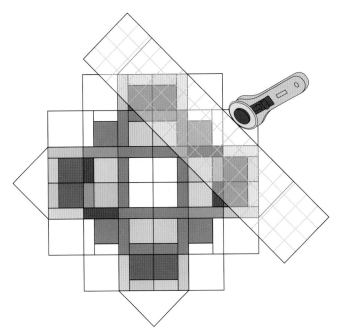

15. Repeat Steps 1–14 to make 3 more large blocks.

Make the Sashings

Note The sashings are cut to this measurement. Adjust for your block as needed. If sewn correctly, the block should measure 25½″ × 25½″.

1. Cut 2 of the 2½″ background strips to measure 25½″ long.

2. Cut 2 more background strips to measure 29½″ long.

3. Sew the 25½″ strips onto opposite sides of the large block. Press the seam allowances toward the sashing.

4. Sew the 29½″ strips onto the remaining sides of the large block. Press the seam allowances toward the sashing.

5. Repeat Steps 1–4 for the other 3 blocks.

Quilt As-You-Go

1. Layer with batting and backing and baste (see Layering Columnar Sections, page 13, and Basting Columnar Sections, page 13).

2. Quilt in quarter section fashion (see Quilting Quarter Sections, page 17).

3. Trim away any excess fabric from the edges of the quilt.

4. Join the sections (see Joining Quarter Sections, page 17) with the center sashing strips.

5. Trim away any excess fabric from the edges of the quilt.

6. Bind the quilt using your preferred method.

Quilt assembly

About the Author

This is Judy's sixth book with C&T Publishing. She is the owner of Bungalow Quilting in Ripon, Wisconsin. She loves scrap quilting most of all, and sewing garments was her original passion. Judy is also a designer for Studio e Fabrics. She teaches at many guilds around the country and at national shows. She has been sewing since age 6 and has credited her success to her 4-H leaders. They not only taught her the right way to sew but made her rip and gave constructive criticism that helped her to grow as an artist. She has been married for 35 years. When she's not sewing or working in the shop, she can be found outside, throwing a ball for her golden retriever, Duncan.

Visit Judy's online and follow on social media!

WEBSITE: Bungalowquilting.com

FACEBOOK: Bungalow Quilting and Yarn

INSTAGRAM: bungalowquilting

YOUTUBE: Bungalow Quilting and Yarn

BLOG: Bungalowquilting.com

CREATIVE SPARK: creativespark.ctpub.com

Photo by On Edge Photography

ALSO BY JUDY GAUTHIER: